# Limited War in the Nuclear Age

# LIMITED WAR

## in the Nuclear Age

Morton H. Halperin

HARVARD UNIVERSITY

John Wiley & Sons, Inc., New York · London · Sydney

THIRD PRINTING, APRIL, 1966

Copyright © 1963 by John Wiley & Sons, Inc.

Library of Congress Catalog Card Number: 63-18625

Printed in the United States of America

To my parents

WRITTEN UNDER THE AUSPICES OF THE CENTER FOR
INTERNATIONAL AFFAIRS, HARVARD UNIVERSITY.

Created in 1958, the Center fosters advanced study of basic world
problems by scholars from various disciplines and senior officers from
many countries. The research at the Center, focusing on the processes
of change, includes studies of military-political issues, the modernizing
processes in developing countries, and the evolving position of Europe.
The research programs are supervised by Professors Robert R. Bowie
(Director of the Center), Alex Inkeles, Henry A. Kissinger, Edward
S. Mason, Thomas C. Schelling, and Raymond Vernon. A list of previous
publications of the Center appears on pages 185–186.

# Preface

THE DEVELOPMENT OF NUCLEAR WEAPONS and intercontinental missiles has ushered in an era in which nations possess the power to
destroy each other completely but in which they have not devised a
way of eliminating violence as the ultimate means of settling international disputes. While idealists and more practical thinkers press the
search for an enforceable method of peaceful change, American and Soviet policy makers have faced the more immediate problem of applying
force or the threat of force in a limited way without bringing on all-
out nuclear war. The dilemma of the policy maker—posed most
dramatically by the events in Cuba in the fall of 1962—is how to apply
or resist force to attain the objectives of the nation without running
undue risks of all-out nuclear war. This is the central concern of this
study.

However the role of force in a period of unlimited power and
ideological conflict poses dilemmas for the analyst of international
politics and foreign policy as well. Certainly no theory of international politics can fail to take into account the new conditions created
by the unleashing of the atom or to explain the phenomenon of states
engaged in a major struggle in which they use some military force
but not those nuclear weapons whose use might be decisive. Though
the policy dilemmas faced by the United States in using limited force
provided the impetus for this study, my aim throughout has been
to grapple with the theoretical problems of an era in which limited
means are used despite the fact that both the United States and the
Soviet Union have vastly greater means of destruction, and the latter
has far-ranging objectives.

Unlike studies of nuclear war which fortunately must concern themselves only with hypothetical events, a study of limited war in the nuclear age can draw on a series of historical clashes in Korea, the Taiwan Straits, Cuba, Indochina, and elsewhere, as well as theoretical speculation about the role of force in the nuclear age. Throughout, my concern has been to combine the two in an effort to explain past events which have involved the use of force with the Soviet Union and the United States on opposite sides, to predict the likely evolution of such future conflicts, and, finally, particularly in the concluding chapter, to distill some recommendations for American policy which emerge from the study. Thus the book is directed not only at military strategists and policy makers but also at students of international politics and foreign policy who hopefully will find the study understandable and relevant to their theoretical and policy interests.

It is a great pleasure to record my debt to the Director of the Harvard Center for International Affairs, Robert R. Bowie, and to Henry A. Kissinger and Thomas C. Schelling, Faculty Associates of the Center, not only for their generous support of my research, made possible by grants from the Rockefeller and Ford Foundations, but also for numerous stimulating and helpful conversations. My fellow Research Associates at the Center, Lawrence S. Finkelstein, Fred C. Iklé, Robert A. Levine, James L. Richardson, and Henry S. Rowen, provided numerous comments and criticisms of earlier drafts of the manuscript and gave generously of their time in rereading revised sections and encouraging me to analyze my arguments.

I have benefited from discussions with the Fellows of the Center at sessions of its Political-Military Seminar and with my colleagues in the Harvard-MIT Faculty Arms Control Seminar. I am also grateful to the following persons for comments on part or all of the manuscript: Donald G. Brennan, Bernard Brodie, Karl W. Deutsch, Tom J. Farer, Allen R. Ferguson, Alexander L. George, Paul Y. Hammond, Samuel P. Huntington, William W. Kaufmann, Charles McCall, Thomas W. Milburn, Ellen G. Moot, Guy J. Pauker, John B. Phelps, Glenn H. Snyder, Kenneth N. Waltz, H. Bradford Westerfield, and Allen S. Whiting.

This book has benefited from related research done for the Hudson Institute, the Institute for Defense Analyses, and the RAND Corporation. My work for these groups and, in particular, a summer spent at the RAND Corporation in Santa Monica have been of immense, if indirect, value in writing this book. Some of the ideas presented here were originally developed in a paper prepared for Project Michelson of the U. S. Naval Ordnance Test Station, China Lake, California.

An earlier version of Chapter 3 appeared in the *Political Science Quarterly;* a version of Chapter 4 appeared in *The Journal of Conflict Resolution;* and a shortened version of Chapter 6 appeared in the *New Republic.* I am grateful to the respective publishers for permission to reprint this material.

Acknowledgments are gratefully made to the following publishers for permission to quote material: Frederick A. Praeger, Inc., for the use of Herbert S. Dinerstein, *War & The Soviet Union: Nuclear Weapons and the Revolution in Soviet Military and Political Thinking* (copyright 1959); the Council on Foreign Relations, Inc., for the use of John Campbell, *Defense of the Middle East* (copyright 1958 and 1960); the University of Chicago Press for the use of Robert E. Osgood, *Limited War* (copyright 1957).

Miss Suzanne Sims not only typed and proofread but also checked footnotes and performed numerous other tasks far beyond the call of duty.

My intellectual and personal debt to Thomas Schelling is far greater than I can hope to express here. From the earliest to the final stages of the project, his criticism, help, and encouragement have been a constant source of inspiration and challenge.

The numerous contributions of my wife, Ina, are all the more remarkable in that she managed at the same time to provide me with a son. David Elliot Halperin arrived today, and I can only hope that this book will in some small way contribute to making this a better world for him to grow up in.

MORTON H. HALPERIN

*Cambridge, Massachusetts*
*November 28, 1962*

# Contents

# Limited War in the Nuclear Age

# 1

# Motives for Expansion and Limitation

WHEN THE UNITED STATES and the Soviet Union have clashed on local military battlefields, they have used far less than all of their military power. They have exercised what Bernard Brodie has called "a deliberate hobbling of a tremendous power that is already mobilized and that must in any case be maintained at a very high pitch of effectiveness for the sake only of inducing the enemy to hobble himself" [42, p. 311].* On a number of occasions in the postwar period the United States and the Soviet Union have clashed directly or by proxy in local areas and have employed force or the threat of force. In Cuba in 1962, in Laos and Vietnam throughout the postwar period, in the Taiwan Straits in 1955 and 1958, in Korea in 1950–1953, in China in 1946–1949, in Lebanon in 1958, in Greece in 1946–1949, and in Berlin in 1948 and in 1958–1962, force or the threat of force has been used in local areas. Each of these was a "local war" (or potential local war), that is, a war in which the United States and the Soviet Union saw themselves on opposing sides but in which the homelands of the two major powers did not come under attack.

Not every war in the postwar period has been a "local war." The Arab-Israeli War of 1948 was one of the largest postwar incidents of violence in which the Soviet Union and the United States never lined up on opposite sides. In other cases Soviet-American opposition has played only a small role in the conflict. In the Suez crisis of 1956, for example, it was only when the Soviet Union made missile threats against Britain and France, and the United States made counterthreats against the Soviet Union, that the crisis became a potential local war. The

* Numbers in brackets refer to items in the bibliography.

1

Congo crisis of the early 1960's, on the whole, has not involved any East-West clash except for the short period when the United States was supporting Kasavubu and the Soviet Union was backing Lumumba. Similarly the Sino-Indian border dispute for a long time was not a "local war" but became one in November 1962 when the United States began to supply military aid to the Indians.

This study deals with "limited war" defined as a military encounter in which the Soviet Union and the United States see each other on opposing sides and in which the effort of each falls short of the attempt to use all of its power to destroy the other. Most of the study is concerned with locally limited war, or what will be called here simply "local war." Much of the military-strategy literature has used the terms "limited war" and "local war" synonymously. However, during the past few years, it has become clear that central war, that is, a war involving attacks on the homelands of the two major powers, may also be limited war. Though most of this study will focus on locally limited war, Chapter 6 will consider the possibilities for limiting central war. The historical materials drawn upon for this study will be from the local wars just cited, almost all of which have involved ground military action in which the Soviet Union and the United States clashed only by proxy. However, as the incidents in the Caribbean in October and November of 1962 should make clear, local war may involve direct clashes between the two major powers and may involve incidents in environments other than the territory of other states. In the future space may provide an arena for limited war.

Because the United States and the Soviet Union have a capability to destroy very large parts of each other's homelands, they share an interest in restraining their mutual destruction in the event of war. It is sometimes argued that this condition makes war obsolete in the sense that we will never have another major war. Demonstrating the necessity for a condition, however, does not demonstrate its possibility, not to say its probability. Even for a number of years prior to the atomic age, it has not been in the interest of a major power to go to war in most situations. Though the development of thermonuclear weapons and intercontinental missiles makes the disutility of warfare even clearer, it by no means eliminates the possibility of war. If war does come the major powers have shared and will continue to share an interest in trying to limit the use of force to something short of the all-out use of their military power in an effort to destroy each other. The existence of thermonuclear weapons and the lack of any mechanism for guaranteeing the absence of war makes it necessary to take seriously the problem of how war, once it erupts, can be kept limited.

The Sino-Soviet threat to the United States makes it even more imperative that the United States develop an understanding of and an ability to engage in limited war. The Sino-Soviet bloc has demonstrated an understanding of the techniques of various forms of local warfare (including guerrilla warfare) as well as a willingness to exploit the use and the threat of force to advance its international objectives. The experience of the postwar period suggests that the United States will continue to be faced with the local use of violence by the Soviet Union, China, and other Communist states and indigenous Communist forces.

Both major powers have shown a willingness to use force and the threat of force when they have felt it necessary to secure vital objectives. In engaging in the local use of force, either directly or by supporting indigenous groups, the major powers have been concerned with avoiding "explosion"—the sudden transformation of a local war into a central war by the unleashing of strategic nuclear forces. In fighting a local war the major powers have been and will be trying to prevent an explosion, but they will also be making a series of decisions about when and how to expand, contract, or conclude a local military encounter. During a local war both sides will be continually assessing the likelihood of an explosion and the question of whether or not they ought to unleash their strategic forces. They will also be assessing the likelihood and desirability of "expansion"—a gradual increase in the level of military force employed.

These two processes, "explosion" and "expansion," are frequently discussed together as "escalation." However it is important to keep the two processes separate. The considerations that go into the decision to begin a central war would be very different from the considerations that have gone and will go into decisions to expand a local war. These latter decisions will be influenced by a number of factors, including the foreign-policy objectives of the two sides, their estimate of the risk of central war, their images of the role of force, and their domestic political objectives. Each of these factors will be discussed to show how it influences the decisions of the major powers during a local war.


## FOREIGN-POLICY OBJECTIVES

The United States and the Soviet Union will have three levels of foreign-policy objectives that will influence their conduct in a local war: basic foreign-policy objectives, political-effects objectives, and battlefield objectives. The desire to avoid central war, which may be viewed as an additional foreign-policy objective, is discussed in the following section.

The basic foreign-policy objectives of the two sides provide the framework in which decisions about the use of particular tools, including local violence, are made. One basic objective of the Soviet Union is to expand the area of Communist control and to reduce Western influence throughout the world. In the long run the Soviet leaders may envision the total Communization of the world. To what extent this long-run objective influences Soviet policy is a matter of much dispute, but there seems to be little doubt of the Soviet leaders' desire to increase Russian influence and decrease Western influence throughout the world. The United States, on the other hand, whatever hopes its leaders may have for an ultimate transformation of Communist society, is committed to seeking to stop the growth of the area under the control of Communist regimes. The Soviet Union, if focusing simply on its objective of spreading the area of Communism, has an incentive to use as much force as is necessary to accomplish this objective, and the United States has an incentive to use whatever amount of force is sufficient to hold the area being attacked. Other pressures, however, will lead the major powers to temper their military efforts to expand their area of influence or to prevent the expansion of the influence of the other major power by force. Within these constraints the leaders of the Soviet Union and the United States will be guided by the political effect they hope to gain by supporting the use of force.

## Political-Effects Objectives

When the major powers participate in a local war it is because of the expected political effects of doing so and not because of the direct pay-off from battlefield success. Neither the United States nor the Soviet Union, for example, has any interest in the small Quemoy and Matsu islands off the coast of China. Nor is the precise parallel that divides North Korea from South Korea something that in itself is worth fighting a war over. It is rather the political consequences of losing or gaining territory that are the major concern of the two sides in committing their forces, their matériel, or their prestige in a local war.

Perhaps the most important political-effects objective with which each side has been and will be concerned in a local war is the message which its conduct will give to its main enemies. The estimates which the leaders of the United States and the Soviet Union have about each other's willingness to use force or the threat of force to secure objectives will be influenced by the conduct of the major powers at any time at which they clash on a local battlefield. In deciding, for example, to prevent the Soviets from establishing a missile base in Cuba, the United States was at least partly motivated by the feeling that it was important to demonstrate to Soviet Premier Nikita Khrushchev that the United States was prepared to use force and risk a nuclear war in order to secure its objectives. The United States acted to convince Khrushchev that the Kennedy administration was not too "liberal" to fight when it felt its rights were threatened.

Another major political-effects objective in a local war is to demonstrate, to other countries in the area, which way the tide is running. The manner in which the United States responds to Communist aggression in Indochina, for example, affects the orientation of Thailand, the Philippines, and other Asian nations. Our willingness to support the Chinese Nationalist Government in the Taiwan Straits has been seen by at least some of our Asian allies as a test of our willingness to support them under pressure. In the same sense the Korean War may be seen partly as a fight over the orientation of Japan.*

Though the ramifications of the outcome of a local war are likely to be felt most keenly in the immediate geographic area of the battle, the implications may also be world-wide. If, for example, the Russians have been restraining the Chinese in the Taiwan Straits for fear of active American intervention, they are likely to be more ready to approve of a Chinese military move if the Western position has collapsed in Berlin. Alternatively, Chinese Communist success in the Taiwan Straits might well embolden the Russians in Central Europe. Soviet success in establishing a missile base in Cuba might have led America's NATO allies to believe that the United States would not defend Berlin.

Even when the battlefield itself may have some intrinsic value, as in the case of Berlin, the political-effects objectives of the two sides will still be more important. It has been clear to at least some Western leaders, since the renewed Soviet effort to change the status of Berlin dating from 1958, that the real Russian objective concerned Germany, the NATO alliance, and the consolidation of Soviet control in Eastern Europe. If the United States uses force over Berlin it will be clearly fighting to maintain the Western orientation of Germany and the cohesion of the NATO alliance as well as to defend the freedom of the West Berliners.

* Chapter 3 is an attempt to apply to the Korean War the model of the limiting process to be developed here and in the following chapter. Thus these chapters will generally avoid examples drawn from the Korean War.

The United States is interested in defending an abstract principle of international conduct—that international boundaries cannot be changed by the use of force. This was a major consideration in dealing with the 1958 Chinese Communist attempt to seize Quemoy. Although the American government may at times have been willing to cede the off-shore islands, it has not been prepared to give them up if this would weaken the principle of no change of boundaries by the use of force. In some situations even when there is no clear violation of international law the United States wants to demonstrate its willingness to commit military forces and matériel, to "act tough" when necessary to defend its allies. In some situations, as in the case of covert aggression in South Vietnam, for example, the United States has had to act to secure this objective in the face of less clear-cut violations of international law. From the Sino-Soviet point of view the aim is to convince nations that the West is not prepared to defend them against either overt or covert aggression and that the wave of the future is international Communism.

These political-effects objectives of the two sides produce pressures to intervene in local-war situations and to expand the level of military effort. However there are other political-effects objectives which tend to work in the other direction.

In contrast to a period of central war when attention will be focused almost exclusively on political and military implications of the "battle-field" encounter and its effects, during a local war the attention of policy makers on both sides will be divided between the particular local encounter and other aspects of the international political struggle. There will continue to be other points of contact and dispute between the two sides. Some of these may be other local wars or situations of potential local war, in which the political-effects objectives will be those tending toward expansion, but at other points of contact one or both sides may be trying to come to accommodation. Each side will be conscious of the possible impact of a local war on its efforts to reach accommodation in other geographic areas or on other problems. In 1954, for example, the Sino-Soviet bloc was about to launch a peace offensive which would have been embarrassed by the continuation or expansion of the war in Indochina. Similarly in 1958 when East and West were beginning to clash over Berlin, they were at the same time attempting to negotiate a treaty to ban nuclear tests. The successful conclusion of these negotiations would have been highly unlikely in the event of armed conflict on the European continent.

Another major restraint on the fighting of a local war will be the reluctance of the major powers to commit resources that may be required to deal with other areas of potential violence or to deter central war. In committing troops to Lebanon in 1958, for example, the United States was faced with the fact that it was thereby reducing its ability to deal with possible violence in the Taiwan Straits; and in 1962 American moves in Southeast Asia must have been restrained by the consciousness of the need to maintain an ability to deter or fight on the European continent. With both sides aware of the possibility of simultaneous or future clashes in other geographic areas, neither will be disposed to commit resources to one local conflict at the risk of dangerously exposing itself at other points. The degree to which this consideration restrains local war depends, of course, on the magnitude of the military action and on the size of the local-war forces of the two sides.

Although the desire to convince other allies that the United States is prepared to defend them produces pressures to use force sufficient to defend the local areas, this objective also generates pressures to use only that force which does not destroy the area being defended. For example, if the United States defended Taiwan by engaging in a nuclear duel with the Sino-Soviet bloc and if this led to the total destruction of Taiwan, it would hardly encourage other nations to seek American defense support. Similarly the initiation of local military action to defend Berlin might cause such devastation in Central Europe as to lead to the disintegration of the Atlantic alliance. To show an ability to restrain the use of violence may be as important as demonstrating a willingness to use violence.

For similar reasons the United States may find it necessary to try to maintain in power the government which was in control at the beginning of the crisis and which called for American support. If the outcome of a local-war situation in which American intervention is invited is always or frequently a change of government, a group in power may seek an accommodation with its enemies rather than accept American support.

The Sino-Soviet bloc on the other hand has an incentive to increase the destruction in a local war fought outside the Communist bloc, in order to demonstrate the lack of utility of American military aid. It also has an interest in a change in government, particularly if the change is from a strongly pro-Western to a neutral government. The Soviet leadership may also be seeking to demonstrate in dealing with a local-war situation that it is prepared to act vigorously to expand the area under Communist control and that it is not unduly afraid of Western counteraction. In its competition with the Chinese for the support of Communist revolutionary groups, the Soviet leadership may feel compelled to expand its intervention to prove to other Communist groups that Russia is prepared to support them when they are close to a seizure of power.

To some extent the policy makers themselves of the major powers will be conscious of the political effects of local war, but in addition both their allies and the neutral nations will continually bombard them with advice, suggestions, and other forms of pressure. Again these pressures may be to expand the war in particular ways or to contract it or to bring it to an end. For example, the United States has received conflicting advice from its SEATO allies as to its policy in dealing with military action in Vietnam and Laos. Beginning in 1954 the British, later joined by the French, have continually opposed proposals for the intervention of SEATO or American forces into the internal wars in Laos and Vietnam. On the other hand, the Thais, the Filipinos, and the Pakistanis have frequently urged a more active intervention by the United States into these situations. More extensive action by the United States in support of the Chinese Nationalists has been opposed by America's European allies.

The ability of allied countries to influence American policy in a local-war situation will in part depend on their general relationship with the United States. The British have exercised a major influence on American local-war policy during the entire postwar period beginning with their transfer to the United States of primary responsibility for aiding the suppression of the Greek Communist rebellion. On the other hand, the extent of the influence of any particular allied country will be affected by whether or not it is actively engaged in the combat. Allied pressure seems to have been most effective in the Korean War when a number of nations joined the United States by committing forces, albeit token ones, in the defense of South Korea. Allied pressure was least important in the 1962 Cuban crisis when the United States was prepared to act alone. The Soviet Union may find that the influence of its Chinese or even North Vietnamese allies increases as they make greater contributions to joint efforts. Though Chinese influence in the present period probably tends toward the use of force, this was not the case in 1956 when the Chinese seem to have counseled a restraint on the Soviets in Poland [343, pp. 55–58].

## Territorial Objectives

Since the battlefield itself is likely to be of little intrinsic importance, territorial objectives in a local war will be determined by the nature of the perceived political effects of different outcomes. Some battlefields such as Western Europe, however, will have significant intrinsic value, and in some cases the loss of a particular area will make it more difficult, for tactical military reasons, to defend nearby areas. A Communist takeover in Laos might, for example, make it harder for the United States to defend South Vietnam and Thailand.

As long as the United States and the Soviet Union confine a war to the territories of other countries, they cannot demand or expect the unconditional surrender of the other major power. However, their objectives may be very extreme, including the ceding of large amounts of territory and the unconditional surrender of the local government; or they may be extremely limited, involving a return to the *status quo ante* or even less. At least at some times, and perhaps at all times, during a local war, both sides will have at least implicitly formulated war-termination conditions, that is, battlefield conditions which if accepted by the other side will lead them to terminate the local conflict. However these war-termination conditions may fluctuate during the war through a range of possible territorial objectives. The territorial objectives, as they are determined by political-effects objectives and other pressures to be discussed hereafter, will be the most immediate determinant of the decision to expand a local war. A side with relatively limited territorial objectives is less likely to find it necessary to expand the scope of its military operations. As each side recognizes the relatively limited objectives of the other, the danger of *explosion* into central war will be substantially reduced. However, even minor objectives may produce pressures to *expand* the war if one or both sides find that their limited objectives cannot be obtained at the level at which the battle is being fought, or if the objectives of the two sides are incompatible.

In addition to the extent of territorial objectives of the two sides, another crucial factor will be whether or not the objectives are specific, concrete, and clearly stated. Although some commentators have suggested that specific objectives clearly stated are more likely to lead both sides to contract rather than to expand a local war, this is not necessarily the case. Certainly if the specific battlefield objectives of the two sides were clearly incompatible, there would be strong pressures toward the expansion of the war. The United States in particular might find it more difficult to compromise if it had clearly stated its territorial objectives than if it had not spelled out its objectives in advance, and if they were in fact flexible. Flexible and moderate battlefield objectives of the two sides are likely to be most conducive to the stabilization, contraction, and termination of a local war. On the other hand, extreme war-termination conditions which expand with success on the battlefield are likely to lead to the expansion of a local war.

The fluctuation of war-termination conditions in a local war will stem in part from the difficulty of assessing the relationship between political-effects objectives and territorial objectives. For example, the United States is not really sure what the impact of a withdrawal from the Chinese Nationalist-held offshore islands would be on its foreign-policy objectives. During the Korean War, the political effect of the stopping of the war at the thirty-eighth parallel clearly would have been different from what it was when it finally occurred if the United States had stopped of its own volition after routing the North Korean army. And no one can really be sure as to the difference in political effect of stopping at the thirty-eighth parallel as opposed to moving to the narrow neck, or seeking to capture all of North Korea. This difficulty of clearly correlating political-effects objectives with territorial objectives is likely in general to be a pressure to expand the local war. When in doubt as to their ability to secure their objectives with particular war-termination conditions, the leaders of a major power may play it safe by expanding their war-termination conditions. Territorial objectives will also fluctuate with military success or failure. The American decision to unite Korea by force stemmed directly from the defeat of the North Korean army. The importance given to defending Taiwan is the result of Communist control of the Chinese mainland. Military success and defeat, and changes in the loyalty of indigenous groups drastically alter the range of possible battlefield objectives.

The role of foreign-policy objectives in influencing the decision to expand or contract a local war, then, may be summarized as follows: unconditional surrender of the other major power is incompatible with local warfare. Neither of the major powers will be seeking in a single local war to implement all of its foreign-policy objectives. The major objectives of the two sides in a local war will be their political-effects objectives, particularly those centering around the legitimacy of the use of force and the need to convince enemies that they will be opposed and allies that they will be supported. Territorial objectives and the war-termination conditions will be shaped largely by the general political-effects objectives although the relationship between the two will not always be clear.

## RISK OF CENTRAL WAR

The desire to avoid central war exercises a major influence on decision makers during a local war. Though this desire is one of the foreign-policy objectives of each side, it is sufficiently critical to require separate consideration. Almost all analysts agree that the fighting of a local war increases the possibility of central war, but it is impossible to determine precisely the extent to which any local war in fact increases the danger of central war. One can, however, envision several ways in which a local war might lead to central war. These include expansion which seems most likely to occur in an important region such as Europe and in a nuclear war. There is also the possibility of an explosion which may occur for one of two reasons. Central war which results from explosion may be an "inadvertent war" that occurs although neither side wants it. It may be the result of pressures to strike first in the event of war which become aggravated as the local war goes on. However central war might also be "deliberate war" resulting from the decision of the losing side in a local war to initiate a strategic strike rather than accept defeat on the local battlefield. If the losing side in a local war considers the area under contest to be of vital significance to it and if it feels that it can win a central war, it might unleash its strategic forces rather than accept local defeat.

It is impossible to make a general assessment in the abstract of the probability that a local war will cause a central war. Certainly there is a widespread belief shared by many decision makers that local wars are dangerous because of the likelihood that they will spark a nuclear holocaust. Whether this danger is as great as decision makers think is less important in this context than the recognition that decision makers will be motivated in the conduct of a local war by their perception of the danger of a central war taking place.

The image which decision makers have of the danger of central war will be determined partly at least by their image of the nature of the strategic balance. In fact, in discussing local wars in any historical period, it is important to specify the nature of the strategic balance, and in particular the image which decision makers have of the balance and their beliefs about how this balance should influence their own and their opponents' behavior in a local-war situation.

Two kinds of questions about the nature of the strategic balance are relevant: How stable is the balance? Is one side more likely than the other to initiate and to win a central war?

The danger of an inadvertent war is greatest in a period in which one or both sides have a strong incentive to strike first if war should occur. In this situation, because strategic forces themselves are vulnerable to destruction by the opponent's strategic forces, one or both sides may see that it is vitally important to be first or at least a close second should there be an explosion into central war. Such a situation might imply two different outcomes of a strategic exchange. The side going first might escape all retaliatory damage. On the other hand, the side going first might suffer significantly less damage than the opposing side and end up winning the war. It appeared to most public military commentators in 1962 that in the late 1950's and early 1960's the United States was in such a position that if it struck first it would probably win and might not suffer extensive damage. On the other hand, in retrospect, it appears in 1962 that the Soviets have never been in that position, although the damage that they might suffer now in the event of central war would undoubtedly be less if they struck first than if they waited for the first blow from the United States.

In this situation, in which the opponents must be sensitive to the possibility of an explosion into central war and to the importance of responding quickly to such an attack, both sides will be constantly concerned with the danger of explosion during a local war. Should a local war occur in a period of strategic instability, both of the major powers will probably seek to minimize their stake in the war so that no outcome will appear to affect their basic relationship in ways that make the danger of an explosion more likely. During such a period, the direct use of combat forces of the major-power countries may seem so risky as to be untenable in almost all local-war situations. With both sides alert to the danger of inducing a preemptive attack, the local war is likely to remain in low key while both sides refrain from expansionist actions such as the introduction of nuclear weapons or the crossing of an international border which will heighten the tension and the expectation that an explosion is imminent. This does not mean that there will be no use of military force, but rather that if one side decides that it must initiate war, it may decide that the only prudent thing to do is to initiate central war or very low-level, ambiguous violence.

Though both sides are likely to feel that it is extremely important to avoid the kind of head-on clash that makes both believe that central war is more likely, the Soviets and the Chinese might find an unstable strategic situation a particularly appropriate one for the kind of ambiguous military actions for which they, in general, seem to have a preference. The optimum strategy for this sort of strategic situation is one which creates for the opponent the alternative of instituting major war or yielding.

While producing powerful incentives for both sides to be cautious, an unstable strategic balance is also likely to provide profitable payoffs for a side willing to take risks. Faced with a *fait accompli*, the defending side is likely to be inhibited from joining the battle in a situation of unstable deterrence. Thus, if local military action does not lead to preemption, it also is not likely to lead to intervention. An unstable strategic balance, then, is likely to reduce the danger of local war and central war by expansion if both sides act cautiously. If both sides try to use an unstable situation as an opportunity to make daring gains, hoping that the other side will be paralyzed by the threat of thermonuclear war, then such a situation may prove to be very dangerous with the world constantly teetering on the brink of preemptive central war.

On the other hand, the initiation of fairly large local war may be one way of signaling to the other side that one does not believe that the strategic balance is unstable, and that one does not believe that there is any danger of preemption. For example, the United States might believe that the Soviet strategic forces cannot be as vulnerable as the Administration thinks they are, if the Soviets are prepared to unleash a fairly large local war.

Beginning about 1957 both sides seemed to have begun to take seriously the possibility of a successful preemptive first strike [69; 102]. Without necessarily having been preoccupied with this danger of preemption, the leaders of the major powers seem to have had and continue to have an appreciation of the possibility of explosion. Among the many other determinants of decision on whether to expand local wars, this general perception of the danger of central war was probably an important factor in keeping down the level of local violence during the past several years.

If and when the strategic balance becomes more stable, that is, when both sides have strategic forces so well protected that there is no perceived advantage in striking first, the effect of the strategic balance will change.

As Glenn Snyder [278, p. 31] and Thomas Schelling [260, pp. 3–4] have pointed out, both sides are more likely to run risks in a local war when they are complacent about the stability of the strategic balance. What will count is the perception that each side has of the likelihood of an explosion. Even if strategic forces are well protected, the leaders of the major powers may continue to believe that the danger of an inadvertent war of one kind or another is still so great that they cannot afford to underestimate this risk in dealing with a local-war situation; they may also believe that the cost of a central war is so great that expansion of a local war must always be carried out with caution because the gains of success in a local war are not worth a large risk of causing an explosion.

Nevertheless it is possible that by the late 1960's we will be in a situation where both sides perceive a very small risk of a local war exploding into central war. The pressure against the expansion of local war may thus be alleviated to such a point that very large local wars involving the territory of a number of states, the armies of the major powers, and the use of nuclear weapons will not be impossible. It is conceivable that a war of the size of World War II would be fought without its expanding or exploding into central war. Certainly a major restraint against wars of the size of Korea will be eliminated when the pressure against expansion, stemming from the fear of an explosion, has been greatly reduced. This very lack of pressure against the expansion of a local war might, unless other pressures intervened, lead to a war which very slowly and gradually expanded to the point where it became a central war. One might imagine, for example, a war on the European continent becoming larger and larger until it led to strategic attacks on the Soviet homeland which were followed by attacks on the United States. In such a war, however, the major powers might still observe a number of important limits including not attacking cities.

Not only is the major powers' perception of the likelihood of central war important, but so also is their perception of what a central war might look like, and specifically, the possibility of one side or the other winning.

Certainly, during the 1950's and, according to recent statements by American defense officials, into the 1960's as well, the United States has had a preponderance of strategic force. Should a war occur, then, the United States could probably expect to win, although the amount of damage that it would suffer in such a war has steadily been increasing. Sometime in the late 1950's the American strategic position vis-à-vis the Soviet Union switched from that of total predominance to relative superiority. Prior to this time, although the Soviets could perhaps have made significant gains in local areas including Western Europe, they could not have inflicted any damage of significance on the United States. At the present time while the United States still apparently has strategic superiority, the Soviets might be able to inflict major damage on the United States even in the event of an American first strike. At present we are in a period in which there remains a premium on striking first and in which there continues to be an American predominance of strategic forces such that the United States is likely to win any central war. In this situation there is strong pressure on the Soviet Union not to expand the level of violence in a local war and not to initiate any kind of local war, particularly one involving a crossing of international boundaries, which might create a substantial danger of explosion. On the other hand, although the United States need not fear losing a central war, American policy makers place a high utility on the avoidance of the damage which would be likely to be inflicted on the United States and Western Europe in such a war. Thus, even given American superiority, the fear of central war will still operate on both sides, albeit perhaps unequally, to generate pressure to contract or end a local war. The relative caution on both sides in dealing with the Laos conflict and in maneuvering over Berlin very likely reflects in part their fear of an explosion into central war.

No matter how stable the strategic balance becomes and regardless of the relative inferiority of one side or the other, the fear of an explosion into central war will exercise major pressures on decision makers on both sides in any local-war situation. These pressures will always be toward the contraction or ending of the war although they will considerably lessen if and when both sides become convinced that the strategic balance is extremely insensitive to pressures from a local-war situation.

## IMAGES OF THE ROLE OF FORCE

The foreign-policy objectives of the two sides and their estimate of the probability of central war will be shaped by their images of international politics and in particular of their image of the role of force. In fact, the very possibility of a local war taking place depends on each side's being willing to engage in such warfare. Since each side now has the capacity to unleash strategic forces which could reach the other's homeland within an hour, only a decision not to use this power—or no decision to use it—if any violence breaks out makes local war possible. The actions of the United States and the Sino-Soviet bloc in the postwar period suggest that their military doctrine is not incompatible in this sense with the fighting of local wars.

This is not to say that a prerequisite of the fighting of a local war is that either or both sides have a clearly defined military doctrine for such a war. Prior to 1957, at least, the United States had no such doctrine and yet it engaged in a number of limited military encounters, including the Korean War. Little is known about esoteric Soviet doctrine on local wars. The Soviets, as will be discussed hereafter, refuse to acknowledge the possibility of international local wars but exalt the possibility of internal local wars or, as they call them, "wars of liberation." Certainly there has been no explicit exchange of attitudes between the United States and the Soviet Union on the possibility of limiting local wars. While such discussions may contribute to the containment of local wars, they clearly are not necessary. It is probably true, however, that a local war is more likely to terminate prior to explosion if there has been such an exchange of views on the problems of preventing central war in a period of local war. If both sides could be made aware of the others' recognition of the need to define limits which prevent the unending expansion of a local war, explosion would be less likely. In addition, if certain possible limits have been discussed, and tacit or formal agreement on them reached, they would more likely serve as the limiting points in preventing the further expansion of a local war. However, if one side wishes for other reasons to expand a local war, perhaps to increase the shared risk of central war, it may have an incentive to expand the war in ways which precisely do break the agreed limits. The discussion of possible limiting points would nevertheless strengthen the presumption on each side that the other did not believe in the inevitability of central war after a clash of East and West on a local battlefield.

There are, of course, major differences in the images of the role of force held by leaders in the United States and those held by leaders of the Sino-Soviet bloc. These differences in image may make the limitation of war more difficult by giving different meaning to the same event.

### Sino-Soviet Images *

In a widely quoted speech delivered on January 6, 1961, Khrushchev discussed three possible categories of wars: world wars, local wars, and liberation wars and popular uprisings. He argued that the Soviet Union already had the military capability to forestall the outbreak of a world war. Turning to the next category, he commented:

There is much talk in the imperialist camp today about local wars, and the imperialists are even making small-caliber atomic weapons to be used in such wars. There is even a special theory on local wars. Is this mere chance? Not at all. Some of the imperialist groups fear that a world war might end in complete destruction of capitalism, and for this reason they are banking on local wars.

There have been local wars in the past and they may break out again. But the chances of starting wars even of this kind are dwindling. A small-scale imperialist war, no matter which of the imperialists starts it, may develop into a world thermonuclear and missile war. We must, therefore, fight against both world war and against local wars [148, p. 50].

Such a local war, he suggested, was the Suez crisis in 1956. He identified the Indochinese and the Algerian Wars as "liberation wars," and stated:

* For more extended discussion, see Dinerstein [69], Garthoff [89], Hsieh [126], Kissinger [159, pp. 316–402], and Zagoria [343].

There will be liberation wars as long as imperialism exists, as long as colonialism exists. Wars of this kind are revolutionary wars. Such wars are not only justified, they are inevitable, for the colonialists do not freely bestow independence on the peoples. The peoples win freedom and independence only through struggle, including armed struggle.

Why was it that the U. S. imperialists, who were eager to help the French colonialists, did not venture directly to intervene in the war in Viet Nam? They did not do so because they knew that if they gave France armed assistance, Viet Nam would receive the same kind of assistance from China, the Soviet Union and the other socialist countries, and that the fighting could develop into a world war. The outcome of the war is known—North Viet Nam won [148, pp. 51–52].

The apparent thrust of Khrushchev's argument is, therefore, to rule out both world wars and local wars initiated by the West, but to proclaim the inevitability of anti-imperialist and Communist-inspired local wars. Thus, when the Soviets proclaim that "limited war" is impossible [294], they mean that Western-inspired local wars are impossible and that the West should not intervene in local wars. The Soviets themselves seem to be ready for local wars and have maintained ground forces capable of fighting both conventional and nuclear ground wars [89]. And, as Herbert Dinerstein has pointed out, the Soviets engaged in a series of limited actions in the past, in Poland and Finland in 1939, in Japan in 1945, and planned the action in Korea in 1950 [69, p. 28].

In all of these cases [Dinerstein continues] the Soviet Union hoped that the employment of limited means would achieve ends proportionate to the effort expended. . . . In the wars against South Korea and Finland the Soviet Union was unable to attain her planned objectives in the time allotted and therefore abandoned the original objectives rather than risk an expansion of the war and an expenditure of resources incommensurate with the ends desired [69, p. 28].

The Soviets have always been willing to use limited force to gain limited objectives which suggests their appreciation of the fact that there is no inherent reason for war to be expanded indefinitely once it occurs.

The affinity of the limited use of force and Communist ideology has been discussed by Nathan Leites, who in the prologue to his *A Study of Bolshevism* points out that one of the motives which may lead to a Soviet initiation of a war is the need to "push to the limit," that is, to take advantage of any power vacuum to extend the area of Communist control. This compulsion may cause the Soviets to start or expand a local war, even when it is not in their long-run interest to do so [174, pp. 27–63].

There is, however, according to Leites, a countervailing Bolshevik compulsion which provides one clue to the failure of the Sino-Soviet bloc to initiate or expand local wars. This is the need to "avoid adventures." Thus the failure of the Soviets to seize Northern Iran or West Berlin and to advance into Greece or Yugoslavia may be explained by their unwillingness to court a disastrous encounter with the United States which would have led ultimately to Soviet destruction. Even when the Bolsheviks initiate a war in order to fill a power vacuum, they are ever prepared to retreat or limit their objectives so as not to engage in "adventures."

The Soviet leadership has an intense dislike for situations over which it does not have control. It believes that it is important at all times to be able to determine the course of events, in particular to have one's own forces under control. This feeling will produce pressures against the expansion of a local war in ways, such as the use of nuclear weapons, which might produce novel situations over which the Soviets might not have control.

The Chinese Communist approach to the use of military force has been largely influenced by this same Marxist approach. The Chinese as well as the Russians view force as an instrument of political policy and have demonstrated in Korea, in Indochina, on the Sino-Indian border, and in the Taiwan Straits an ability to use limited force to secure particular political objectives. The original contribution of Mao Tse-tung has been in the development of guerrilla-warfare strategy [195], and the Maoist guerrilla strategy has been applied with success in Indochina [295]. The Chinese have sought to export the revolutionary technique to other countries of Southeast Asia and throughout the underdeveloped areas.

The differences on local war between the Soviet and Chinese leaders have not been over their image of the general role of force in international relations, but concern the specifics of the current historical period. The Soviets seem to take much more seriously than the Chinese the danger of an explosion from local war to central war. They may also have a greater appreciation than the Chinese of the destruction which their respective countries would suffer in the event of a strategic attack from the United States. Thus the Chinese seem in principle to be more prone to encourage local war and to support local Communist forces. In particular the Soviets seem to argue that the danger of central war is too great relative to the gains from local revolution to justify an adventurous policy [343, pp. 245–276].

The Chinese and the Soviets have disputed the appropriate strategy to be followed in particular countries. For example, the Chinese propose to support revolution in India, and the Russians want to cooperate with the "bourgeois" government. While this pattern seems to hold for most of the underdeveloped countries, in some (for example, Cambodia) the Soviets seem more anxious to promote revolution. By and large the lower estimates by the Chinese of the danger of explosion into central war, and their greater faith in the efficacy of revolutionary warfare, have led them to exert pressure on the Soviets to expand their aid to local Communist revolutions.

## American Images *

There is, of course, no single American image on the role of force in international relations. Nevertheless one can, as Osgood [223] has done, identify the predominant approach of Americans to the role of force in international affairs as being hostile to the notion of limiting the use of available force in war. This tradition, which at least until very recently dominated the approach of American policy makers, has looked on war and peace as two distinctly separate states. War has been viewed not as a continuation of policy but as a failure of diplomacy. It has been believed that when war comes military factors and the military must dominate. The American response to war has been to view it as the use of force in a great moral crusade in which there is no room for the deliberate hobbling of American power. If war is viewed as part of a continuing power struggle, then the limiting of war makes sense. However, viewing war as a moral struggle, it is difficult for most Americans to be sympathetic to the concept that it must be fought according to certain "rules" and that it involves cooperation with the enemy.

Americans traditionally have not viewed war as a legitimate instrument of offensive action. War could be used to defend certain rights when they were being challenged by force, but not to implement American political objectives. Violence has been seen as an unnatural part of international politics which would be eliminated by the observance of international law and by disarmament. The American approach to war has been much more hospitable to attempts to abolish rather than to limit violence. The development of American strategies for the limited employment of forces has been opposed by two groups which share a fundamental unwillingness to accept violence as an inevitable part of international politics. At one extreme have been those

* For more extended discussion, see Osgood [223] and Tucker [313].

who insist that to talk about limiting war is to block the path to total disarmament.* And at the other extreme are those who argue that to limit the use of force in military warfare is disastrous since a war must be fought to total victory and the unconditional surrender of the opponent if the world is to be made safe for peace-loving nations. Attempting to control war suggests a compromise: a willingness to engage in violence without the expectation that it will bring all warfare to an end or radically transform the nature of international politics, and a willingness to engage in a war which is admittedly part of a long-run political, military struggle.

Writing in 1957 of the dilemma brought on by the need to control warfare and the fundamental American opposition to this concept, Robert Osgood noted:

> The record of the United States does not show a real adjustment, either in its underlying conceptions of force and politics or in its concrete policies, to the imperatives of a strategy capable of resisting limited aggression by limited means. Such an adaptation is bound to be encumbered by the weight of traditional habits of mind resisting the pressure of unprecedented events [223, p. 45].

Osgood's book and the writings of many others have been a plea for a change in the American approach. Nevertheless his basic conclusion will remain valid; even though the general American attitude moves toward a willingness to accept the necessity of attempting to control the use of violence in the nuclear age, American attitudes will continue to be shaped by this historical commitment to the belief in war as a moral event. On the one hand, this image will produce pressures to stay out of particular local wars which clearly cannot be viewed in terms of a moral crusade and which are in no sense "wars to end war." On the other hand, once the United States enters a war, there will be pressures to expand the conflict and to seek a decisive victory.

There is another strand in the American approach to war which will produce pressures toward intervention in any military conflict. This is the belief most clearly evident in the actions of Secretary of State John Foster Dulles that force should not be used by any nation to change its international boundaries. For example, in the Taiwan Straits in 1958, the United States opposition to the Chinese Communist seizure of the

---

* The objections to limiting war in many ways parallel the current objections to "arms control." Both arms control and "limited war" are attempts to live with the reality of international violence and international disputes, and to reduce their danger in an era of nuclear weapons. To the total disarmer this approach interferes with the task of outlawing war, for he assumes that war can never be controlled—it must be abolished.

offshore islands was publicly justified largely in terms of the principle of the non-use of force. The rationale for this doctrine is provided at two levels. On the one hand, it is argued that the moral principle should be observed for its own sake. On the other hand, it is argued that if the United States permits an aggressive, totalitarian nation to seize one piece of territory by force, that nation will never be satisfied until it meets a greater counterforce. Thus, if force is not opposed at once, it will have to be dealt with later when it is even more menacing. This belief in the need to stop the expansion of the area controlled by international Communism by the use of force has provided the major justification for American involvement in local wars. This approach also militates against more than defensive objectives in a local war. It was from this perspective that many Americans argued that the United States should have stopped at the thirty-eighth parallel in the Korean War and which at the present time inhibits the extension of the Indochina guerrilla war into North Vietnam. War in this view is fought with the single purpose of returning to the *status quo ante*. If this cannot be obtained at a particular level of violence, there will be intense pressures to expand the level of violence. On the other hand, once the objective has been obtained, force, in this view, should no longer be applied.

## Evolution of American Images

Because of these traditional American images of the role of force, the need for a capability and a doctrine for fighting local war has been accepted only slowly and reluctantly by Americans in the postwar period. Even with the end of the dream of American-Soviet cooperation, it was assumed that the danger from international Communism lay either in cold-war subversion or in a "total" war which would begin by a massive ground attack in Europe. Slowly over the course of a decade and a half officials, analysts, and a wider American public have recognized that the Sino-Soviet bloc is capable of posing a variety of military threats including local ground action. Consequently an understanding has developed of the need to have a capability for dealing with the dangers of the overt and covert local use of force. This intellectual evolution has been influenced not only by a series of major historical events in the postwar period but also by intensive study of security problems by civilian and military analysts.

Just prior to the Korean War there was some discussion in the United States of certain aspects of local warfare. A joint State Department-Defense Department committee had begun to consider possible uses of force by the Soviet Union short of a massive strike on the European continent [108]. And prior to this the Truman administration had given massive aid to Greece in a successful effort to put down a Communist-inspired internal revolution; American aid to Nationalist China, however, had not prevented the spread of Communism to China.

Despite Greece and China the Korean War for the first time brought home dramatically to the American public and American policy makers the possibility of engaging in military clashes with the Soviet bloc which would not resemble World War II. Without any clear understanding of the problems of this kind of warfare, the Truman administration nevertheless turned pragmatically to the task of meeting the North Korean aggression.

In 1951 at the Senate hearings into the dismissal of General Douglas MacArthur, the American people were presented with their first full-scale debate as to the acceptability of limiting warfare. The hearings revealed not only that there was very little understanding even on the part of the Truman administration as to the nature of the struggle in which it was engaged, but also the frustration with which a large part of the American public and policy makers had reacted to the Korean War [199].

Although the Eisenhower administration in ending the Korean War was determined to avoid similar encounters, it came close in 1954 to committing American troops to the defense of French Indochina [188]. At the same time the Administration was depending on the policy of "massive retaliation" which recognized the possibility of local aggression but attempted to avoid a dependence on local defense as the main option with which to meet this threat. In his "massive retaliation" speech of January 12, 1954, Secretary of State Dulles argued that "there is no local defense which will alone contain the mighty manpower of the Communist world. Local defense must be reinforced by the threatened deterrent of massive retaliatory power" [71].

The speech led to much criticism of the policy of massive retaliation and, in fact, was the catalyst which produced the first large volume of "limited-war" literature in the United States. However neither the Dulles speech nor the Eisenhower administration's policy in general reflected a rejection in principle of the necessity for local-defense forces. Rather the Administration was saying that it was not prepared to support local-war forces large enough to deal with all possible aggressive acts of the Sino-Soviet bloc. Therefore local ground defense had to be reinforced by the threat to use America's strategic nuclear power. At the same time the Administration sought to make up for its manpower inferiority by the adoption of a tactical nuclear strategy [281]. The course set in 1954 was followed through the end of the

Eisenhower administration in 1961. Ground forces were held down in size and converted as quickly as funds would allow toward a position in which they would be able to fight only by using tactical nuclear weapons. Even on strategic forces the Administration spent less than its critics proposed, but its emphasis was on the development of America's nuclear striking power for the deterrence both of direct attacks on the United States and of local aggression.

However the Administration's doctrine as reflected in its speeches and budgetary decisions seemed to have little relation to its action policy. In 1954 in Indochina the Administration considered not massive retaliation but the introduction of American tactical air and ground forces [188]. In 1955 and 1958 the United States exercised great restraint in dealing with Chinese Communist threats in the Taiwan Straits. American policy was to supply the Chinese Nationalists with forces to deal with the crisis and to refrain from any overt nuclear retaliatory threats [311]. In Lebanon in 1958 the Administration in its show of force used only ground forces with nonnuclear equipment [31].

In the closing days of the Eisenhower administration, the Indochina crisis flared up again, creating the possibility of local warfare in both Laos and Vietnam. Again it was clear that only conventionally armed soldiers could intervene in a decisive way in the confused guerrilla-warfare situations. But it was perhaps in Berlin—the other crisis which the Eisenhower administration turned over to its successor—that the policy of trying to defend local areas by strategic retaliatory threats was most in evidence. The Eisenhower administration, in effect, seemed to rule out the possibility of defending Berlin by ground action.*

The Kennedy administration brought into office a number of individuals who were convinced of the need to build larger conventional forces for local defense. They were faced immediately with the crises in Indochina and Berlin which strengthened their conviction and led to the decision to improve and enlarge the conventional capability of American and, hopefully, allied armed forces. At the same time, partly because of President Kennedy's interest in guerrilla warfare, increased attention was given to developing a capability for dealing with internal wars for which conventional military formations are not entirely appropriate. Thus the lower end of the spectrum of violence—conventional regular warfare and irregular warfare of various kinds—has been emphasized by the Kennedy administration.

There is not, then, any single American image of the role of force in international politics. The images of Kennedy, Dean Rusk, and Robert McNamara, for example, differ from each other and from the

* See Eisenhower Press Conference in *New York Times*, March 12, 1959, p. 12.

images of Eisenhower and Dulles. The impact of these images on American policy in a local-war situation can only be precisely determined by considering the image of the policy makers who at that time are shaping American policy. Nevertheless their image will always be applied against a background of hostility to limiting the use of violence by those in the political opposition and in the general public who have a different approach to the use of force.

## DOMESTIC POLITICAL OBJECTIVES

The fighting of a local war is not likely to bring an end to domestic politics in the United States or the Soviet Union. In Russia those domestic pressures which affect foreign policy are likely to operate with equal force during a period of local war. The leadership group will remain concerned with preserving its ascendancy and with domestic objectives, including the growth of the economy. However the impact of domestic politics-as-usual is likely to be greater in the United States. Foreign-policy objectives will to some extent conflict with domestic political objectives, and the conduct of the United States will be influenced by the need to balance foreign and domestic objectives.

A local-war period will contrast with the central-war situation in which we can expect domestic politics to come to a halt and in which the conduct of the war is put outside the pale of legitimate political criticism. The extent to which politics-as-usual continues will depend on the size of the local war and the extent of American involvement. A large war in Central Europe involving U. S. and Soviet troops would probably bring an end to domestic criticism. During most local wars, however, American policy-making will remain exposed to domestic political pressures, and other actors on the political scene, including military officers, will feel free to criticize and to seek to influence the decisions of the Administration on the conduct of the war. Some, particularly those who believe that war should never be limited, will be pushing for the expansion of the war. There will be other domestic political pressures supporting the Administration's acceptance of moderate war-termination conditions in local warfare.

It is probable that the Administration will view a decision to intervene with combat forces in a local war as entailing great domestic political costs. There seems to be a general belief that the Korean War substantially hurt the Democratic Party at the polls in the succeeding years. This belief is likely to influence an American President's decisions in future local-war situations and did have some impact on the Kennedy administration's approach to the Laos crisis in 1961–1962, particularly in its reluctance to expand the war by introducing American troops. It can be expected that a decision to introduce American troops will be a difficult one for any President concerned with his own and his party's political future, in view of the American casualties and the frustration that will result.

Once the American government commits combat forces, or major aid short of that, as it did in Vietnam in 1962, to a local war, there will be pressure to see the war through to decisive victory. Echoes of the view of General MacArthur that there is no substitute for total victory, at least on the local battlefield, are likely to be heard during any local military encounter. Any hobbling of power which prevents the decisive local victory will generate intense domestic political pressures. There will also be somewhat contradictory pressure to end the war as quickly as possible. During the Korean War there was pressure on the government either to expand the war or end it. There seemed to be very little objection in 1953 to the decision of the Eisenhower administration to bring the war to a close without a victory. What will prove most unpopular domestically will be the continuation of fighting without a clear-cut decision.

The decision to expand a local war will be influenced not only by the reactions of other political actors and the American electorate, but also by the major domestic goals of the Administration itself, on which its political life also depends. The Kennedy administration is anxious to forward the domestic goals of the New Frontier in housing, education, health, and so on, and will be aware that its commitment of American troops and matériel to a large-scale local war might interfere substantially with its ability to advance its domestic welfare programs. In addition, during a local-war period, the American President must give attention to the impact of his actions on his own prestige and his own power, as they affect his domestic political image.

# 2

# Interaction between Adversaries

IF NEITHER MAJOR POWER wants a total war, but both are prepared to support the use of force by an indigenous group or to employ their own force, local wars can take place. If the net results of the factors discussed in Chapter 1 lead the major powers to initiate or to support the use of force in local areas, there will be interaction between the two sides, complicated by the role of independent indigenous forces and influenced by the pressures discussed, to establish the limits on the war and to determine the battlefield outcome. The process of interaction between adversaries in a local war is complex and confused. General principles can only provide a framework in which to understand and analyze interaction in a particular local-war situation.

## INITIATION

In 1960 the attempted coup d'état of the heretofore unknown Captain Kong Le began a new phase of violence in the complicated Laotian civil war. The consequences of his action led to an East-West confrontation at a formal conference at Geneva and to a local war. As Thomas Thornton has pointed out, however, "the initial coup of Captain Kong Le took both Moscow and Peking by surprise, and the entire course of events since then gives the impression of having been improvised" [307, p. 501]. The initiation of a local war may then be the result of actions of indigenous forces aligned neither with international Communism nor sympathetic to the West. Local war might also be initiated as a result of even more spontaneous action (for example, riots

26

in East Germany). The decision to initiate a local war, or a revolution which becomes a local war, may be made by local Communist forces without necessarily securing the approval of the Soviet Union. This appears to have been the case both with the Chinese civil war [343, p. 12] and with the Vietminh rebellion in Indochina after World War II [295, p. 4].

Thus the motives influencing the actions of the two major powers may be irrelevant to the outbreak of local violence. On the other hand, in the Korean War and the series of Communist uprisings in Asia in 1948 [307, p. 497], the Soviet Union apparently deliberately ordered the initiation of the use of violence in order to expand the area of Communist control. The attempted Cuban invasion of 1961 suggests that the United States might be capable of initiating local warfare.

The initiation of local war may be a sudden break between peace and violence, but it is more likely to be bridged slowly by relatively low levels of military action. The 1958 Taiwan Straits crisis, for example, resulted from stepping up the level of Communist artillery fire on the offshore islands which had occurred regularly for several years. The eruption of fighting in Indochina in 1961 and 1962 was simply the intensification of guerrilla action which had been carried on since the end of World War II. In fact, with the exception of the Korean War which went directly from very minor border skirmishes to a major conventional war, the initiation of large-scale local war in the postwar period has been almost imperceptible in the sense that the transition from minor violence to local war has occurred relatively slowly and with very small increases in the use of force. The situation becomes a local war, according to the definition being used here, when the major powers recognize that violence is taking place in which they are on opposite sides.

## EXPANSION

The process by which the major powers are drawn into a situation of local violence will depend largely on the way in which the violence breaks out and the nature of the local forces involved. When, as in the Taiwan Straits, one side is a Communist regime and the other an ally of the United States, the involvement of the two major powers is immediate and evident. At the other extreme, in the Congo, for example, where the local forces involved were relatively unknown and diffuse, the commitment of the major powers to the two sides occurred slowly and lasted for only a brief period when the Soviets supported Lumumba. The pressure for intervention is likely to be derived mainly from the perceived political effects of the possible course of events with and without major-power action. Pressure for American intervention is likely to come, as it did in Korea, in Indochina in 1954, and in Lebanon and in the Taiwan Straits in 1958, from civilian rather than military officials. This results from the lack of intrinsic military value of these territories and the political implications of defending them. As George Modelski has pointed out, some involvement of the major powers in protracted local violence is almost inevitable since at least the weaker party in the local struggle will be seeking outside aid [200]. Once they see themselves involved in local violence, the major powers must decide on the degree of their participation or at least the degree to which they wish to commit themselves at this point.

Short of direct participation of combat troops, the major powers and other countries can permit volunteers to fight in the war or they can clandestinely supply personnel as the North Vietnamese appear to be doing in South Vietnam. Outside powers can supply matériel ranging from rifles to nuclear weapons and can help to train military personnel. The "training" can extend, as is presently the case with United States aid to the government of South Vietnam, to on-the-spot advice to troops engaged in combat. The most modest form of intervention is support in diplomatic channels and the United Nations of the kind, for example, that the Soviets provided to the Chinese Communists during the 1958 Taiwan Straits crisis.

In addition to the limits on the degree of participation of the major powers and other countries outside the area of combat, possible constraints on the level of local war may involve limits on geography, types of weapons systems, and types of targets. These limits may be quantitative or qualitative. One side, for example, may use none of its planes or it may use some of them; one side may bomb none of a particular class of targets or it may bomb some targets in that class, but not others. In the local wars which have taken place in the postwar period, both qualitative and quantitative limitations of geography, kinds of targets, and kinds of weapons have been observed by the major powers and their allies.

## BATTLEFIELD INTERACTION

In deciding whether or not to expand a war, the major powers will be concerned with the battlefield implications of their action. The initial pressure for the expansion of military activity is likely to come from the perception that such an increase in the level of violence will improve the military outcome. It seems to be the case, at least for the United States, that in previous local wars, expansion in the level of violence has resulted from the desire of the military to take actions which would improve the battlefield situation. In none of the analyses of particular past local wars is there any indication that expansion, after the initial decision to intervene, was implemented except when the military proposed it. The decision to intervene in Korea, for example, was made by civilian officials with the Joint Chiefs declining to offer an opinion. From then on, however, pressure for expansion originated with the field commander or the Joint Chiefs. The same pattern seems to apply to the other local wars in which the United States has been involved. To what extent this is also true on the Soviet side is not known.

Although the question of expansion may be raised for tactical military reasons, the decision ultimately is made on the basis of the conflicting pressures on decision makers, including this need to improve the tactical military outcome. In considering the possible improvement of the tactical military situation by the expansion of a local war, the possibility of an enemy response needs to be taken into consideration. There is no reason to assume that every expansion of a local war will lead to a counterexpansion. However, before expanding a local war, each side must at least consider the possibility of an enemy response. The enemy's reaction to a particular expansion may be to take the same action; however, if this option is not available, the opponent might expand the war in a different way. That there will not always be a response even to qualitative expansion is indicated, for example, by the failure of the Chinese Communists to implement any counterexpansion to the use of Sidewinder air-to-air missiles by the Chinese Nationalists over the Taiwan Straits in 1958. However, since counterexpansion is possible and in some situations perhaps likely, the decision maker must analyze the situation with the two changes, that is, the initial expansion by one side and the reaction by the other. The side contemplating expansion must decide whether the move is in its interest from the point of view of improving the battlefield outcome and of its other objectives.

It is also necessary for the side considering expansion to evaluate the possibility that once the particular limit being observed is broken it may become impossible to prevent the continuous expansion of the war until no limit is being observed (at least in that particular category of limitation). For example, in considering bombing a small strip of Chinese territory in response to Communist intervention in a local war, the

United States must consider whether this means that both sides will ultimately engage in very extensive bombing operations against each other's territory.

Schelling [257, 259, 261] has developed a model of tacit bargaining which illuminates the process by which the two sides seek to establish limits on a local war by bargaining over acceptable stabilization points. He attempts to explain the establishment of those limits which both sides recognize that they have agreed to and which are observed because of the belief that no alternative limits to expansion are possible.

Tacit bargaining, according to Schelling, takes place in a situation in which communication is incomplete or impossible. "The problem is to create a modus vivendi when one or both parties cannot or will not negotiate or neither would trust the other with respect to any agreement explicitly reached" [257, p. 19]. The problem, then, is to explain how in these circumstances agreements are reached. According to Schelling, without communicating with each other, both sides maneuver to establish agreement on certain kinds of points as particularly appropriate limits of a local war. Since successful bargaining requires agreements on limits, the essence of success in this situation is to establish the legitimacy for the kinds of limits that one wants to have.

Schelling's model is most applicable to those situations in which a limit is in fact established as a result of each side being preoccupied with coming to an agreement with its opponent on a particular limit. The need to maintain the particular limit may be based on the belief that there is no other possible limit short of central war. The reluctance of both major powers to use nuclear weapons in local wars, for example, is based partly on the fear that no other limit on the use of nuclear weapons could be found. The decision not to break a limit may also be based on the belief that this particular act of expansion might lead to some counterexpansion and, even if the war is then stabilized, the tactical military situation will not have been improved. For example, the possibility of Chinese Communist intervention in Vietnam in response to United States intervention has deterred American action in the belief that this double intervention would make the tactical situation worse from the American point of view.

In addition to the tacit or explicit bargaining about particular limits in a local war, there may be more general and diffuse bargaining between the two sides on the level of their efforts. Each side may recognize that the other is exercising massive restraint on its available military resources and that each would respond in some way to an expansion by the other. The bargaining here may not be over particular limits but rather over the effectiveness of the military capability employed. The

Chinese Communists in 1958 may have believed that the United States would respond to any military action on their part which threatened the offshore islands. Similarly, what appears to have brought the Chinese into the Korean War was American success on the battlefield and not any single expansion in the means employed. Simultaneous with the bargaining over particular limits aimed at preventing undesired expansion or explosion, then, will be tacit negotiation over battlefield objectives and war-termination conditions which will influence decisions on expansion.

Many decisions on expansion will be affected by levels of bargaining as well as the general pressures discussed in Chapter 1. The degree of influence of bargaining considerations will vary, and in some cases its role may be insignificant. For example, many of the decisions made by the United States in the Korean War, including the quantitative limits on American manpower and weapons, were based on the desire to maintain an adequate capability to defend Europe and to strengthen the Western Alliance and not on the fear of enemy reaction to expansion of the war. Domestic pressures as well may account for particular limits. The decision of the United States not to intervene in Indochina may be attributable in part to President Eisenhower's reluctance to act without the support of Congressional leaders and his failure to gain that support. In other cases, such as the use of nuclear weapons, the need to arrive at a particular limit as well as the more general bargaining may reinforce pressures extraneous to the interaction against the crossing of the nuclear-nonnuclear line.

The role of the bargaining process described by Schelling will thus vary in importance from decision to decision and from war to war. In some situations both sides may be extremely conscious of the interaction between them and the need to agree on limits. In such situations their actions may conform closely to the predictions implied in Schelling's model. At the other extreme, in some situations both sides' attention may be focused away from the battlefield, and there may be little appreciation of the need to coordinate in order to prevent expansion or explosion. Most situations will be in between: decisions on expansion will be made with some attention to bargaining in general and over specific limits, and with some attention to the pressures arising from the world-wide obligations and objectives of the major powers.

In any case, unless there is an explosion, the process of expansion will continue until both sides decide that it is not in their interest to expand the war. This point needs emphasis in view of the contention of many analysts that a war can be kept from expanding only if the side losing the tactical military battle has no incentive to increase the level of violence. This belief apparently is based on the premise that both sides prefer to fight at the lowest possible level and that only the side dissatisfied with the outcome on the local battlefield would want to expand the military operations. However, although both sides may desire to avoid the economic cost of employing greater military power, there is no reason to believe that only the losing side might expand the war. The winning side might alter its war-termination conditions in ways which require an expansion of the war. The United States, for example, after routing the North Korean army decided to expand the ground war to all of Korea and to seek its unification by force. In 1955 in Indochina it was clear that both sides had to make the difficult decision of whether to continue the war. The West had to decide whether to expand the war in order to rescue a defeated French military force; the Vietminh and its Chinese and Russian allies had to decide whether to press for the unification under Communist control of all Indochina. It was only because both the winning and losing sides agreed not to expand the war that the limiting points of the conflict were stabilized at a level of very low violence.

The greatest probability for expansion is likely to occur at the time of the outbreak of a local war or at a period when one side achieves a clear tactical superiority within the established limiting conditions. There will then be pressure on the losing side to expand the war in order to reverse the battlefield decision and pressure on the winning side to expand its war-termination conditions and hence its military operations.*

Schelling has suggested that the limits which are in fact observed in a local war "may depend on analogy, precedent, accidental arrangement, symmetry, aesthetic or geometric configuration, casuistic reason-

---

* Just as the stabilization of a local war results from a variety of pressures on both sides, so the termination of a local-war situation will not be the result of any single pressure. There is nothing inherent within the logic of local war which determines the time or conditions of war termination. It is rather the broader political-effects objectives of the major powers as filtered through the decision makers' image of the world and their domestic political goals which determine when a war is brought to a halt. The Soviets and Chinese, for example, may have been willing to accept a truce in Indochina in 1954 partly because they thought continued fighting would interfere with the world-wide peace offensive they were about to launch. The war-termination conditions of a local war are determined by the ability of each side to use effectively the force it has available and is prepared to commit and the sentiments and actions of the indigenous population. This last factor may in fact be the critical determinant, particularly in internal warfare.

ing, and who the parties are and what they know about each other"
[257, p. 21]. To the degree that limits are determined by the process of
tacit bargaining, Schelling suggested the points of agreement may be
"obvious" in that they occur to both sides as "legitimate possible points
of agreement" and "distinct" in that the point is somehow qualitatively
different from those surrounding it [257]. In a later discussion, Schelling suggested that most of the points which served to keep a war limited
are "legalistic," for example, the difference between Russians and Chinese, between nuclear and other weapons, between Americans and Nationalist Chinese, between ten miles on one side of the Yalu and the
other, or between the two sides of the Greek-Yugoslav border [259].

Although it is an exaggeration to assert as Schelling has that "limits
are no good if they can't be recognized by both sides" [260, p. 14],
it is probable that limits are likely to be more stable if they are recognized by both sides. If both we and the Russians acknowledge the
difference between American planes flown by French pilots and American planes flown by American pilots, then the distinction is an important one and is likely to contribute to keeping a war from expanding. A number of limits which have been observed in local wars have
conformed to Schelling's suggested qualities of being distinct, obvious,
and "legalistic." Nevertheless, even when limits do arise from bargaining between the two sides, the point may not be qualitatively distinct
and may not be symmetrical. The difference, for example, between
using and not using American combat forces in war is not as sharp as
it may appear. American participation can run a gamut from the use
of all sea, air, and ground forces to the provision of a few "technical
advisers" for the training of indigenous forces. Although there are some
qualitative break points along this line, there is no single clear and predominant one—American activity in South Vietnam in 1962 was erod-
ing even the pretense of a clear line between "combat forces" and
"advisers." However, even where a line does not really exist, the preten-
tion that there is one, the fiction shared and accepted by both sides
that the distinction exists and is being observed, may create a possible limiting point for a tacit bargain. The tacit bargain may, as already suggested, be simply a general recognition of the need for
restraint. Hence the limits observed may be quantitative ones, as for example, the percentage of American fighting forces which was committed to the Korean War or the number of planes which the Russians
would turn over to the Chinese for operations in the Taiwan Straits.
But limits which do not derive from the bargaining situation between
the two sides are perhaps even less likely to be based on distinct and

obvious points.* Many limits will be blurred in the sense that both sides feel restricted in what they can do, with neither absolutely clear as to what the rules are which the other is following or the enemy's image of the restraints that they are observing.

In some cases, in fact, a point which is distinct and obvious may turn out to be less acceptable. For example, in the American march north during the Korean War, the obvious limiting point of the Yalu River turned out to be an unstable limit in that the Chinese Communists' foreign-policy objectives did not lead them to accept a Western military power moving up to its borders. However, as will be suggested in the following chapter, it might be that bringing the Western military advance to a halt at some arbitrary point part way up the peninsula, both by posing less of a threat to Chinese objectives and by posing a greater military challenge in their attempt to roll back United Nations forces, might have provided a satisfactory limiting point which would have prevented Chinese Communist entrance into the war. This possibility of quantitative as well as qualitative limits applies to all four categories of limitations listed previously. As has been suggested, the degree of participation of other states in a local war may be based on the qualitatively distinct points such as no participation versus total participation or on such points as the distinction between combat troops and advisers which both sides pretend are real. The limit, however, might simply be a quantitative restraint on the number of troops employed. Limitation on the geographic area of the war is most likely to be marked by legal boundaries. Many local wars, in particular those which have been confined to the territory of a single country, have in fact been confined within legal boundaries.* However, other geographic limits are possible, as indicated by the fact that the Communist rebellion in South Vietnam reportedly on occasion spills over into Laos. The military encounter in the Taiwan Straits in 1958 involved artillery fire against a strip of China close to the Straits. The geographical limit, if not legalistic, may nevertheless be qualitative and be based on geo-

---

* However, insofar as the limits are based on negotiations with allies or domestic groups, they may in fact have the same characteristics. America's allies, for example, are likely to find it easier to object to a qualitative expansion—to the use of nuclear weapons or the introduction of combat forces—than they are to object to an increase in the number of machine guns supplied to South Vietnamese troops or to the number of American combat forces committed in a local war.
* Many of the local wars which have been limited to the territory of a single country have involved guerrilla and counterguerrilla operations. The limiting process discussed here is applicable to guerrilla as well as more conventional kinds of warfare; however, no specific attention is paid here to the particular problems of counterinsurgency operations.

graphic divisions such as a river or mountain range. But as in some of the examples cited, the geographic limit may be neither legalistic nor geophysical. In these cases, it may be based on the desire to observe limits on targets, weapons, or the participation of states. For example, the geographic restriction imposed on the Chinese Nationalist and Communist activity in the Taiwan Straits seems to have been determined by the decision to restrict the weapons used largely to artillery fire. The range of attack on the mainland was then the range of the weapons employed. In general, it is likely to be true that limitations in one category derive from decisions about limitations in others.

The major weapons limitation that has been observed in local wars involves the qualitative distinction between atomic, biological, and chemical weapons on the one hand and conventional high explosives on the other. However other weapons limitations have been observed. Submarines have not been used extensively, if at all, in local wars, and the major powers have frequently supplied to their allies limited quantities of particular weapons, short of their total capacity to supply these weapons.

Target limitations of various kinds have also been observed. For example, in the Korean War both sides exercised various kinds of target restraints within the North Korean peninsula. Here again the limitation may be qualitative in that, for example, no cities are attacked, or quantitative in the sense that some, but not all, of a particular target comes under fire.*

Thus the restraints which are observed in a local war have been of various kinds. Some have been reciprocal and based on qualitative distinctions resulting in distinct and obvious limits understood and tacitly agreed to by both sides. At the other extreme some restraints have been simply quantitative and have not resulted in sharply defined limits based on tacit agreement or common understanding. Other things being equal, qualitative points based on legalistic reasoning and precedent are most likely to prove to be stable limits. However, other things are seldom equal, and the limits which prove stable will be those which each side determines  are in its interest, regardless of their intrinsic qualities. The necessary condition for the stabilization of a local war is agreement within the decision system of each side—and not agreement between the two sides—that further expansion is undesirable.

* While target limitations of various kinds have been observed in local wars in the postwar period, much of the attention to this problem has been given in relation to the possibility of a local war, possibly a nuclear local war, on the European continent in which target limitations would be critical if damage is to be kept down to tolerable levels.

## PREVENTING EXPLOSION

In order for a local war to stabilize, both sides must decide not to expand and also not to launch central war. It is thus necessary to explore not only the way in which decisions are made about expansion and the kinds of limits which are most likely to stabilize the expansion of a local war, but also to consider the way in which explosion is avoided. One must ask, for example, not only why the Indochina conflict ending in 1954 did not lead to the use of atomic weapons or American troops, but also why it did not lead to central war. These are different, if related, questions.

Explosion will be influenced by whether or not particular limits on expansion are observed. The limits which prevent explosion will be the ones which each side has come to expect will be observed either in local wars in general or in the particular local-war area. For example, in the continuing low-level military battle in the Taiwan Straits, both sides have established the principle that artillery fire on the territory held by the other is acceptable. However apparently neither side has engaged in bombing on the other's territory. To break this limit now or in a future crisis would seem much more serious than if both sides had gradually become used to bombing as they have to artillery fire. The sudden crossing of a previously established limit in a particular local war will force the other side to consider what kind of response it will make —and it will probably feel compelled to make a response. Moreover, both sides will need to ask themselves whether this new local war could be brought to a conclusion without explosion. This uncertainty will produce pressures for preemption.

In addition to limits which have come to be accepted by both sides for the local war in which they have been observed, a number of more general limits have been observed in all or most of the local wars in the postwar period and have made a major contribution to reducing the danger of explosion. These are: the nonconfrontation in battle of American and Soviet troops; the confinement of the theater of war to a single country; the recognition as sanctuaries of supply lines and training zones outside the battlefield area; and the non-use of nuclear weapons.

There is no reason to assume that as soon as Soviet and American troops meet in combat one or both sides would launch their strategic forces. Nevertheless it is true that the use of both Soviet and American troops would destroy one of the most important limits which both sides have come to recognize and which has prevented the explosion of local wars. In general this limit has been carried even further. Not only have the United States and the Soviet Union avoided direct confrontation of their military forces, but also, except in a very few instances (for example, Korea, Hungary), the major powers have avoided the commitment of their own troops. The Chinese Communists as well have been reluctant to commit their own combat forces in a local war.

None of the local wars in the postwar period has covered a very large geographic area. In fact, most of them have been confined to a very small piece of territory, in most cases within the bounds of a single country. The confinement of the war to a small area has frequently left both sides with a sanctuary of supply lines leading into the battle area and of troop training and rest zones. For example, in the current conflict in South Vietnam, the sanctuary of North Vietnam seems to be recognized by the United States and the South Vietnamese forces. In the Korean War, mainland China, Japan, and Okinawa functioned as sanctuaries. In addition to the recognition of particular sanctuaries, supply lines including sea routes leading into the area of fighting have not come under attack by plane, by surface ship, by submarine, or by mines. Again there is no reason to assume that the expansion of a local war to a wide geographic area or attacks on sanctuary and supply routes would make explosion inevitable. However, the breaking of the qualitative limit which has seen most local wars confined to a single country (or at most to two adjacent countries) would again, because of the uncertainty, make explosion more likely.

Perhaps the most dramatic and most important restriction which has been observed in every local war since World War II, however, is the failure of both sides to use nuclear weapons. This should not be taken to mean that explosion is inevitable if nuclear weapons are used. However, as will be discussed in detail in Chapter 4, it is true that a nuclear war is more likely to explode than is a conventional one.

To the extent that the major powers now understand that a war fought with the qualitative limitations just discussed can be brought to a halt without explosion, the incentive to preempt and hence the likelihood of an explosion will be low. The first time that any of these limits are breached or there is some other unprecedented action (for example, fighting on the Central European front) there will be a heightened danger of explosion into central war precisely because neither side can be certain that the war can be brought to a halt without the eventual use of strategic nuclear forces. How serious this is will depend on the degree to which both sides are conscious of the danger of preemption.

In addition to the fact that expansions of various kinds undertaken for other reasons may heighten the danger of explosion, one or both sides may deliberately raise the shared risk of central war. As Schelling has pointed out, one side may feel that the situation is going so badly and that defeat on the local battlefield is so intolerable that the only alternative is to take particular measures—expand the war, alert its strategic forces, and so on—which increase the danger of inadvertent central war [265]. Such measures would not be taken, of course, in the hopes of actually bringing on central war but rather to use the threat of increasing the probability of such war to force the other side to back down. However, these actions may bring on the central war that neither side wants. Alternatively, if the strategy fails to force the other side to back down, or if it appears too likely to bring on a preemptive attack by the other side, the losing side in a local war may conclude that the consequences of defeat are so great that it has to unleash a central war.

# 3

# The Korean War: A Case Study

THE KOREAN WAR was the most nearly direct Soviet and American clash on a local land battlefield in the postwar period, and the only local war in which regular American combat forces were employed. That the Soviets had instigated and supported the North Korean attack was accepted at least tacitly by both sides. There are many characteristics of the Korean War which differentiate it from other past and possible future local wars, but it illuminates the hypotheses presented in the previous chapters.

## FOREIGN-POLICY OBJECTIVES

Prior to the outbreak of the Korean War, the United States believed that a major objective of the Soviet Union was to expand the area under its control. Thus, in responding to the North Korean attack—which had not been anticipated—American objectives were developed in the framework of the belief that the attack was part of a general plan for expansion and perhaps a prelude to general war [199, pp. 942, 954, 971, 2585, 2630]. The United States sought to prevent the success of this Communist attempt to expand by the use of force in the belief that allowing the Soviets to succeed in Korea would encourage aggression elsewhere. General Omar Bradley expressed this purpose at the Mac-Arthur hearings in describing Korea as "a preventive limited war aimed at avoiding World War III" [199, p. 154]. President Harry Truman later described his objectives in intervening in the Korean War in similar terms:

Communism was acting in Korea just as Hitler, Mussolini, and the Japanese had acted ten, fifteen, and twenty years earlier. I felt certain that if South Korea was allowed to fall Communist leaders would be emboldened to override nations closer to our own shores. If the Communists were permitted to force their way into the Republic of Korea without opposition from the free world, no small nation would have the courage to resist threats and aggression by stronger Communist neighbors. If this was allowed to go unchallenged it would mean a third world war, just as similar incidents had brought on the second world war [310, p. 333].

The defense of Korea was partly motivated by the feeling that the action was necessary to convince the West Europeans that the United States would come to their aid. The Administration was wary of committing its military power, thereby leaving itself exposed to Soviet aggression in Europe. During the latter stages of the Korean War, in fact, the major American buildup occurred in Europe and not in the Far East. The Administration was also aware of the danger of splitting the NATO alliance in a dispute over Far Eastern policy. A major objective throughout the war was to prevent adverse repercussions in Europe while using the episode to strengthen NATO and build up its military capability [310, p. 387]. America's NATO allies, particularly the British, constantly applied pressure on the United States to prevent expansion of the war and to bring it swiftly to a conclusion. Following an almost inadvertent reference by President Truman at a press conference to the possibility of using atomic weapons, British Prime Minister Clement Attlee flew to the United States to confer with Truman and to propose the seeking of a cease fire in Korea to be followed by the admission of Communist China to the United Nations [310, pp. 395–413]. Partly because the defense effort in Korea was carried on under UN auspices, the United States felt obliged constantly to consult its allies on policy and was influenced by their continuous efforts to halt the expansion of the war and to bring about its conclusion.

Soviet objectives were more closely related to the situation in the Far East. The Soviets were interested in the capture of South Korea for its own sake and probably expected a relatively quick and easy North Korean victory [329, p. 40]. In addition, the Soviets probably hoped to prevent Japan's alignment with the Western powers. Allen Whiting has suggested the nature of the Soviet Far Eastern objective:

In view of the multiple pressures directed at Japanese foreign policy, the Communist leaders may have conceived the Korean War as serving ends beyond the immediate control of the peninsula. Military victories in Taiwan and Korea could be heralded as ushering in the Communist era in Asia, and as demonstrating the impotence of America's "puppets," Chiang Kai-shek and Syngman Rhee. The resultant effect upon Japan might swing opportunistic groups behind existing neutralist opposition to Yoshida and prevent his supporting American policy [329, p. 37].

This interpretation of Soviet strategy in the Korean War was offered by John Foster Dulles right after the North Korean attack. Dulles, who was at the time the State Department planner for the Japanese Peace Treaty, suggested that the Korean attack may have been motivated in part by a desire to block American efforts to make Japan a full member of the free world. He conjectured also that the attack may have been ordered because the Communists could not tolerate the "hopeful, attractive Asiatic experiment in democracy" that was under way in South Korea.*

The Chinese objectives in entering the Korean War were also based on general political considerations, but of a defensive nature. According to Whiting the Chinese also hoped to influence the course of United States-Japanese relations [329, pp. 156–157]. Moreover they were worried about the loss of prestige they would suffer if they allowed the Western "imperialists" to march unhindered to their borders. And they were perhaps most concerned with the beneficial effects of United Nations success in Korea on the many opponents of the Communist regime still active in China and on Taiwan. Whiting concluded:

In sum, it was not the particular problems of safeguarding electric-power supplies in North Korea or the industrial base in Manchuria that aroused Peking to military action. Instead, the final step seems to have been prompted in part by general concern over the range of opportunities within China that might be exploited by a determined, powerful enemy on China's doorstep. At the least, a military response might deter the enemy from further adventures. At the most, it might succeed in inflicting sufficient damage to force the enemy to compromise his objectives and to accede to some of Peking's demands. Contrary to some belief, the Chinese Communist leadership did not enter the Korean War either full of self-assertive confidence or for primarily expansionist goals [329, p. 159].

The Chinese apparently entered the war with the aim of saving at least some of North Korea. Their minimal objective was to preserve the identity of Communist North Korea rather than its total territorial integrity [329, p. 155].

In an effort to secure the political effects discussed, American battlefield objectives and war-termination conditions underwent considerable fluctuation during the course of the war. When the United States first intervened, its objective was simply to restore peace and the South Korean border [310, p. 341]. Very early in the war and after the Chinese intervention, the United States considered a total withdrawal

* *New York Times,* July 2, 1950.

from Korea [330, pp. 429–431, 438]. Later its battlefield objective expanded to include the unification of Korea. But in the end, the United States accepted a truce line which closely approximated the *status quo ante*. As Richard Neustadt has pointed out, Truman's original decision to seek the unification of Korea failed to take into account the political-effects objectives that the United States was pursuing, and in the end the recognition of this forced the abandonment of the unification effort.

Had the unification of Korea been Truman's dearest object, its announcement as a war aim would have been another matter. But it was among the least of the objectives on his mind. In July and August 1950, in December after Chinese intervention, in his struggles with MacArthur, and thereafter through his last two years of office, his behavior leaves no doubt about the many things he wanted more than that. He wanted to affirm that the UN was not a League of Nations, that aggression would be met with counter-force, that "police actions" were well worth their cost, that the "lesson of the 1930's" had been learned. He wanted to avoid "the wrong war, in the wrong place, at the wrong time," as General Bradley put it—and any "War," if possible. He wanted NATO strengthened fast, both militarily and psychologically. He wanted the United States rearmed without inflation, and prepared, thereafter, to sustain a level of expenditure for military forces and for foreign aid far higher than had seemed achievable before Korea [211, p. 126].

Once the Soviets recognized that they could not easily secure their objective of demonstrating American weakness and unwillingness to use force, they seemed to have abandoned the battlefield objective of capturing all of Korea. They may have been willing to accept an end to the war with part or perhaps even all of North Korea in Western hands, and ultimately settled for a virtual restoration of the *status quo ante*.

## RISK OF CENTRAL WAR

The Korean War was fought before the era of intercontinental ballistic missiles and fusion weapons. Thus, while both sides could have expanded the war quickly and decisively, there was not the danger that now exists of a sudden unleashing of nuclear missiles which within an hour could destroy a large part of both the United States and the Soviet Union.

Even without this threat of a mutually devastating strategic exchange, the danger of a world war was nevertheless present, and both sides seem to have been determined to prevent its occurrence. Truman has reported that the major American aim in Korea was to prevent a third world war [310]. The Russian decision to remain out of the war seemed to be partly motivated by a fear of igniting a global war. In this situation where neither side could gain a decisive advantage by going first, both sides seemed to recognize that, no matter who started the global war, both would suffer major losses. Though the United States could have attacked the Soviet Union with its very limited stockpile of atomic weapons, it probably could not have prevented a Soviet ground attack in Western Europe which might have resulted in Communist domination of the European continent. The Soviets had almost no capacity to attack the United States and could not have prevented an American attack on the Soviet Union. Though both sides avoided forcing the other into starting a global war, neither was constantly concerned with the possibility of "preemption" by its adversary.

The United States, however, was concerned that the Korean War should not lead it to expend those military capabilities which were considered an important deterrent to general war. In Korea the United States was employing the troops and the matériel which it felt were necessary to deter general war. At the MacArthur hearings, Air Force General Vandenburg rejected a senator's suggestion that the United States should commit a major part of the American Air Force to the Korean War effort. He argued instead that the United States must get a cease fire

without endangering that one potential that we have which has kept the peace so far, which is the United States Air Force; which, if utilized in a manner to do what you are suggesting, would [sic.], because of attrition and because the size of the Air Force is such and the size of the air force industry is such that we could not still be that deterrent to [general] war which we are today [199, p. 1385].

Soviet action during the war, including the failure to commit combat forces, suggests that they shared with the United States the desire to avoid a global war.

## IMAGES OF THE ROLE OF FORCE

The North Korean attack on South Korea suggested the willingness of the Communists to seek a limited objective by a limited use of force. The Soviets probably intended to seize South Korea with the use of North Korean forces and then to halt their military operations. When the United States intervened, they recognized their miscalculation of American intentions, but proceeded on the assumption that American intervention need not lead to world war. The attack into South Korea, moreover, seems to have been motivated by the Soviet compulsion to fill power vacuums. In view of the specific United States declaration that South Korea was outside its defense perimeter, the Soviets reasonably could have counted on a quick and easy victory by the North Koreans [329, p. 40]. But, while Communist conduct during the war reflected a doctrine that included the limited use of military force and limited objectives, neither the Chinese nor the Russians seemed to have any idea of the optimum methods of communicating intentions and capabilities to the other side in the course of such a war.

American images of the role of force, on the other hand, seem to have been much less hospitable to the limitation of warfare. It would appear that the United States had not foreseen the possibility of Soviet military action in South Korea or any other local area unconnected with a general Soviet military offensive. The result was the American decision not to prepare for the defense of South Korea in view of the low estimate of its value in a general war. Thus the decision of June 1950 to defend South Korea was not based on a reestimate of South Korea's military importance, but on a recognition that something had occurred for which American military doctrine had not been prepared [199, p. 1110]. In making its policy decisions throughout the war, the United States was operating without any general theoretical notions of the nature of local war in the atomic age, and its decisions were probably affected by the lack of such theory [106, pp. 2–3].

Each side's image of the other's intentions influenced its decisions. The Soviets clearly underestimated the likelihood of American intervention. In the Soviet view American action in withdrawing its troops from Korea and the American declarations that it would defend South Korea only as part of its United Nations obligations had meant that the United States would not in fact defend South Korea. The Soviets failed to anticipate the partly moral and partly political American reaction to aggression. They were insensitive to the importance that the United States would attach to repelling "illegal" aggression, as opposed to less clear-cut violations of international law.

The American decision to intervene in Korea and the subsequent decisions were also based on and influenced by estimates of Soviet intentions.* In assessing the motives of the North Korean attack, American policy makers gave consideration and, to some extent, credence to five different interpretations, as follows:

1. The "diversionary move" interpretation. In view of the number of other areas, particularly Western Europe, that appeared more militarily

* This discussion of the American image of Soviet doctrine is based on George [95].

significant than South Korea, the North Korean attack was seen as a diversionary move, aimed to draw American resources away from the areas where they were most important. Truman reports that he shared this view in part and was determined not to leave Europe vulnerable to Soviet aggression [310, p. 437].

2. The "soft-spot probing" interpretation. By this image of Soviet doctrine, the Soviet compulsion to fill power vacuums had led to the attack on South Korea which had been abandoned by the United States and which was clearly incapable of defending itself.

3. The "testing" interpretation. This was the view that seemed to influence most Truman's image of the North Korean attack [310, p. 333]. It recalled the progress of Hitler's aggressive moves and asserted that the North Korean attack should be seen as a prelude to attacks in other areas if that aggression were allowed to succeed. This view differed from the "soft-spot probing" interpretation in its assumption that the Communists' success in Korea would encourage them to attempt aggression in the other areas where Western defense capabilities were far stronger. In short the purpose of the Korean attack was to probe the firmness of Western intentions, and not simply to fill a power vacuum.

4. The "demonstration" interpretation. By this interpretation, the Soviets were mainly concerned with demonstrating their own strength and American weakness in order to promote, on a long-term basis, important shifts in political allegiance throughout the world.

5. The "Soviet-Far-East-strategy" interpretation. This interpretation put emphasis on the idea, already discussed, that the Soviets hoped to prevent the entrance of Japan into the Western camp and to pave the way for further Communist expansion in the Far East.

As George has pointed out, the inclination of American policy makers toward the "testing" interpretation of Soviet doctrine—in which the Korean attack was equated with Hitler's early expansionist moves—may have reinforced the likelihood that the United States would intervene in Korea. If the "soft-spot probing" interpretation of Soviet conduct had been accepted instead, the United States might have been more prone to cede South Korea while taking steps to prevent the existence of power vacuums elsewhere. The belief that successful aggression would embolden the Soviets made the defense of South Korea seem crucial [95, p. 220].

## DOMESTIC POLITICAL PRESSURES

During the Korean War the Truman administration continued to pursue its domestic political goals. Despite the war there was politics-as-usual on both sides of the political fence. The President was constantly concerned with promoting his Fair Deal program, consolidating the position of the Democratic Party, strengthening his northern and western liberal support in Congress, and calming the political crises raised by such men as Senator Joseph McCarthy [211, p. 126]. Nor was the Administration immune to criticism from the Republican Party, which felt that it was possible, necessary, and desirable to attack the Administration's conduct as well as to question the basic concept of limiting war.

After the MacArthur hearings, a Republican minority report declared:

We believe that a policy of victory must be announced to the American people in order to restore unity and confidence. It is too much to expect that our people will accept a limited war. Our policy must be to win. Our strategy must be devised to bring about decisive victory [199, p. 3590].

These few sentences suggest a number of important assumptions about the nature of wartime politics. The first is the notion that the unity of the American people can be achieved only with a declaration that victory is the goal. A further implication is that, after such a declaration, the method of achieving a battlefield victory becomes a "military" problem that is beyond the realm of partisan domestic politics. On the other hand, once the government admits that there are other political considerations that affect and moderate the goal of a strictly military victory, then, according to this Republican statement, it is legitimate to criticize the particular policy adopted. Unity will come only when the country is asked to back an absolute goal. If there is no such goal, then the opposition has a duty to examine and critically appraise the war effort.

Congress, as a whole, also felt itself free to criticize. The hearings into the firing of General Douglas MacArthur were striking in that they required the Administration, *during the war*, to justify its conduct and to explain what it hoped to accomplish in the war and how the war was being conducted, as well as to explicate a host of particulars which must have been of as much interest to the Communists as they were to the senators across the table. Actually the hearings provided a unique and invaluable opportunity for the Administration to communicate what it wanted to communicate to the Chinese and the Russians. However the senators' questions at this hearing did not have that motivation. Congress forced the Administration to discuss its strategy and objectives during the war without any apparent consideration of the effect this would have on the American war effort.

The quotation from the report of the Republican senators also reflects the then still strong American opposition to fighting a local war. The Senators stated flatly that the American people would not accept a strategy of limiting war, and indicated their rejection of the strategy as well. The implication is that during a local war the American government will be subjected to attacks from the political opposition, from Congress, and from public citizens on two grounds: the legitimacy of fighting such a war and the particular strategy employed in the war.

The general public seems to have shared the Republican senators' dissatisfaction with the course of the Korean War, at least in its later stages. On the other hand, the public apparently approved the decision of the Eisenhower administration to end the war short of victory as it had approved the initial decision to intervene. The public's frustration with the continuing war probably added to the margin of Eisenhower's victory in 1952; his ending the war enhanced the Republican image as the party of peace and increased the Eisenhower plurality in 1956. The Korean War does not seem to have had a major or lasting impact on popular political attitudes [53, pp. 49, 50, 527, 546, 555]. In this respect, American political leaders seem to have overestimated the effect of the war on the voting public. Korea is taken as demonstrating—as to some extent it did—that extended local wars which cannot be decisively won are not popular with the American public. Leading the United States into a major local war or expanding the war without securing a clear victory is likely to be perceived as a political liability; ending a war on almost any terms may be a political asset.

All these domestic pressures undoubtedly influenced the manner in which the Truman administration conducted its Korean operations, both by hampering its freedom of action and by increasing the costs of various actions.

## ATOMIC WEAPONS

The most dramatic limit on the Korean War was that neither side used its atomic weapons. According to Brodie [42] there were four reasons why these weapons were not used by the United States:

1. The Joint Chiefs of Staff and civilian policy makers continued to feel that the war in Korea was basically a Soviet feint. There was, therefore, a strong case for conserving the then relatively limited stockpile of atomic weapons for the principal war which, they thought, would come in Europe. Their fear was not that the employment of nuclear weapons would lead to an expansion of the war and a Soviet

attack on Europe, but rather that Korea was deliberately designed as a decoy to get the United States to exhaust its nuclear stockpile and conventional military resources so that the Soviets could later attack with impunity in Europe. It was the desire, then, to save resources and not the fear of provoking the enemy that was one of the main causes of the American decision not to use nuclear weapons in Korea.

2. American policy was also affected by the reports of local Air Force commanders that there were no suitable targets for atomic weapons in Korea. While the impact of this view was considerable, it apparently reflected an uninformed attitude about the possible uses of atomic weapons. Commanders in the field came to think, for example, that atomic bombs were of little use against bridges, a belief which Brodie explained as follows:

This odd idea probably resulted from a mis-reading of the results at Hiroshima and Nagasaki. Some bridges were indeed badly damaged at those places and some were not, but for the latter it was generally forgotten that a bridge only 270 feet from ground zero at Hiroshima was actually 2,100 feet from the point of explosion, and also that it received its blast effect from above rather than from the side [42, p. 319n].

Nuclear weapons were still relatively new and had not been extensively tested, and it is probable that commanders in the field were too busy to search out potential targets for nuclear weapons.

3. American allies, particularly the British, were strongly and emotionally opposed to the use of atomic weapons in the Korean War [310, pp. 410–411]. This pressure from allies strengthened America's own anxieties and moral doubts about again using these weapons.

4. A subsidiary reason for the failure to use atomic weapons in the Korean War was the fear of the retaliatory employment by the Soviets of the few atomic weapons in their possession against Pusan or Japan, despite the American near monopoly of these weapons. Brodie doubts, however, whether this fear played a conscious part in the relevant decisions [42, pp. 319–321].

The first two motives just discussed will not be important in the future. The American stockpile of tactical nuclear weapons is now so great that military commanders may urge their use precisely because they are a nonscarce military resource, and certainly no argument can be made that they should not be used because they are scarce. Military officers now have a much better understanding of the capabilities of nuclear weapons, which, moreover, now come in much smaller packages. Thus it will be clear to military commanders that there would be suitable targets for their use in any conceivable future major limited war. While we can expect continued pressure from our allies against the use of nuclear weapons, certain allies might advocate their use in some situations. There will, however, be other international political pressures—for example, from the uncommitted or neutral states—against nuclear weapons, and the possibility of a Soviet nuclear response will be a much more important determinant of the decision.*

We know much less about the details of the Russian decision not to use atomic weapons in Korea. The Russians seemed determined not to supply any matériel to the forces fighting in Korea which could clearly be labeled as having been supplied by them after the war began. This would certainly be the case with atomic weapons.† In addition, the Soviet stockpile of such weapons was so small that its use in a localized military encounter might have seemed wasteful.

The limit observed by both sides seems not to have resulted from an attempt—or even an awareness of the need—to bargain with the enemy. However the Soviets were probably more restrained than the United States by the fear that the initiation of nuclear attacks would be met by a response in kind.‡

The Chinese Communists seem genuinely to have feared the possibility of the American use of atomic weapons when they intervened in the Korean War. According to Whiting the Chinese felt that a nuclear response was a real possibility; intervention was considered risky and every effort was made to delay it and to minimize its consequences. The extent of this Chinese concern was reflected both in its shelter-building program and in domestic Chinese Communist propaganda. But Peking was reassured by the three-week testing period of relatively small Chinese intervention which revealed that United States aircraft, though authorized to bomb the Korean ends of the Yalu bridges, were forbidden to venture into Chinese territory [329].

The background of the limit on the use of atomic weapons in the Korean War, then, suggests a failure of both sides to understand what the other side was likely to do and what the other side's fears and goals were. It also suggests that, to a large extent, the determination of limits is based on considerations other than those that result from the battle-

* For a discussion of the factors which should be weighed in considering the use of nuclear weapons, see Chapter 4.

† It was also true, however, of the MIGs which the Soviets supplied probably with Russian pilots.

‡ However, if the use of atomic weapons had been confined to the Korean theater—that is, if the decision to use these weapons was not coupled with a decision to expand the war in some other way—it is not clear who would have gained from an atomic exchange.

field interaction. Some of the other limiting points established in the war reveal the same pattern.

## CHINESE INTERVENTION

One of the major expansions of the Korean War was the decision of the United Nations Command to cross the thirty-eighth parallel. This decision was based partly on the military consideration that one could not stand by and allow the enemy forces to regroup for renewed attack just beyond the border, but also on political grounds—when the battlefield conditions changed in its favor, the United States decided to pursue the unification of Korea by military means. In crossing the parallel the United States was aware of the risk that it might trigger Chinese Communist intervention, and tried by reassuring statements to prevent it. But it apparently underestimated the Chinese reaction and, at the same time, failed to develop a concurrent strategy which, by retaliatory threats or other sanctions, could succeed in preventing Chinese intervention. As Whiting has suggested the threat to use atomic weapons on the Chinese mainland if the Chinese intervened might have been a much more effective deterrent than the attempt to reassure them that a march to the border did not presage an attack on mainland China [329, p. 162].* The threat to use atomic weapons would have involved major political costs for the United States, and the American government might not have threatened to launch an atomic attack even if it had recognized that the threat might be effective. Had the Administration been aware of the fact that the fear of greater expansion might have deterred Chinese intervention, an alternative course might have been to threaten to expand the war to China with conventional weapons. But even this was not done. In fact, a decision was made before the intervention that Chinese intervention would not lead to conventional bombing beyond the Yalu. MacArthur reportedly believed that this decision had been leaked to the Chinese [330, pp. 455–456].

In choosing, instead, to inform the Chinese of its limited objectives, the United States also considered it important to reassure the Chinese that their hydroelectric plants would not be jeopardized by a march up to the Yalu. But, as Whiting has pointed out:

It was widely believed in Western circles that a determining factor in Chinese Communist concern over North Korea was the reliance of Manchurian industry upon power supplies across the border as well as along

* Panikkar, the Indian ambassador in Peking, reported that the Chinese expected an atomic attack, but were nonetheless prepared to intervene [230, p. 108].

the Yalu River. This belief prompted explicit reassurances from Western spokesmen, both in Washington and at Lake Success, concerning "China's legitimate interests" near the frontier. Yet we have seen that Peking ignored this issue completely in its domestic as well as its foreign communications. The absence of propaganda about the protection of the hydroelectric installations, despite the need to maximize popular response to mobilization of "volunteers," suggests that this consideration played little if any role in motivating Chinese Communist intervention [329, pp. 151–152].

In its advance through North Korea, then, the United Nations Command was attempting to communicate two points to the Chinese Communists: first, that it was prepared to go up to but not beyond the Yalu; and second, that it was prepared to respect China's legitimate interests in the northern regions of North Korea. The United States sought, therefore, to establish its limited objectives: that United Nations forces would take all North Korea, that the North Korean government would cease to exist, but China's legitimate industrial interests would be protected. An effort was made to assure the Chinese that the capture of North Korea would not be used as a springboard for an attack into China. The United States assumed that the limits were ones that the Chinese were interested in, and that these limits would serve to keep the Chinese out of the war. But Chinese interests were different and could only be satisfied by different boundary conditions to the war.

Neustadt argues that the Chinese were not in any way affected by the announcement of the United Nations' aim to destroy the North Korean government.

To judge from what the Chinese said, and later did, Peking's concern was with MacArthur's military progress, never mind its foreign policy objective. Chinese concern was not confined to anything so simple as a buffer zone along the border; an entity called North Korea, not the border, was at stake (perhaps in roughly the same sense that South Korea, under reverse circumstances, was for Washington). Even had the UN promised restoration of an independent North once all resistance ceased—which, naturally, no one proposed—I know of nothing to suggest that Peking would have withheld intervention. The communist world does not take kindly, it appears, to the dismantling of a member state's facilities for governance: the party and the army. MacArthur's military progress threatened both, no matter what came after. In short, the military risks and diplomatic dangers usually associated with MacArthur's march across the parallel existed independent of the words used in the UN resolution. MacArthur's march was authorized before the words were seen, much less approved, at Lake Success [211, p. 125].

Washington was apparently convinced even in retrospect that its declarations did not influence the Chinese decision to enter the war and that no other declaratory policy could have altered the Chinese decision.

American policy makers concluded that once the decision was made to cross the thirty-eighth parallel, nothing could be done to affect the Chinese decision. In fact, the State Department reportedly argued in December of 1950 that the Chinese decision to intervene was made prior to the crossing of the thirty-eighth parallel. In one sense, at least, this conclusion may be wrong: the Chinese position might have been altered by threats to expand the war with the use of atomic weapons against China. Moreover it is by no means certain that the Chinese were concerned with the preservation of the total territorial integrity of North Korea. As Whiting suggests an American commitment to advance only part way up the peninsula—that is, to permit the maintenance of the North Korean government in some part of its territory— might have been sufficient to deter the Chinese entrance into the war.

Neither before nor during the first three months of war [Whiting wrote] did the degree of interest in Pyongyang evinced by Peking warrant acceptance at face value of its concern for a "just" peace, based upon the *status quo ante bellum*.

This is not to say that the Chinese Communist leadership was prepared to accept with equanimity the total defeat of North Korea. As a minimal goal, intervention must have been attempted to preserve an entity identifiable as the DPRK, and to prevent unification of all Korea under U.N. supervision. The late date of Chinese Communist entry into the war suggests that it was the political importance of the North Korean government, rather than its territorial integrity, that was at stake. Although intervention was officially predicated upon U.N. crossing of the thirty-eighth parallel, no Chinese People's Volunteers and Democratic People's Republic of Korea defense lines were established during the August-October period, not even to protect Pyongyang. To Peking, a "just" Korean peace was not an end in itself but rather a means towards fulfilling other related goals of policy [329, pp. 155–156].

Thus, even after the crossing of the thirty-eighth parallel, Chinese intervention might have been prevented had the United States acted differently. Although trying to impose limits on expansion, the United States failed to grasp adequately either the reasons that the Chinese felt intervention was necessary or the threats that might have deterred their intervention. Both sides expanded the war, the United Nations by crossing the thirty-eighth parallel and the Chinese by entering the war. Each side failed to convey to the other the kind of counteraction to be expected which might have deterred expansion. China attempted to prevent the crossing of the thirty-eighth parallel by declaring her intention to intervene, but this intention, relayed by the Indian ambassador, was not taken seriously by the United Nations Command [230, p. 111]. The United Nations sought to prevent the Chinese entrance, not by threatening a further expansion but by attempting to satisfy the Chinese security interests that, it was assumed, might lead her to enter the war.

## PORTS AND TROOPS

Despite the fact that United States planes, taking off from airfields in South Korea and Japan and from aircraft carriers, consistently bombed targets in North Korea, the Communists engaged in almost no bombing south of the thirty-eighth parallel. This was one of the major asymmetries of the war both from a legalistic point of view and in terms of interfering with the military operations of the enemy. Both sides apparently devoted considerable attention to the question of what targets to attack, and a variety of motives affected the relevant decisions.

The American decision to bomb targets in North Korea was made prior to the commitment of American ground troops in June 1950. A month later permission was given to bomb industrial targets in North Korea, but the use of incendiary bombs was not allowed because of the civil damage that would have resulted. The Air Force was not authorized to bomb areas close to the Soviet and Chinese borders. Rashin was the single industrial center within the forbidden area and it was the only industrial target in North Korea which was not destroyed by mid-September when an end to strategic bombing was ordered by the Joint Chiefs [85, pp. 174–186]. Not until June 1952 were attacks on the hydroelectric plants in North Korea authorized; within two weeks almost 90 per cent of the North Korean power capacity was destroyed [85, pp. 449–452].

American attacks on targets in North Korea steadily expanded. The attacks were aimed at affecting the immediate military situation. The restraints observed had several motives: (1) to avoid extensive civilian destruction considered undesirable on both humanitarian and propaganda grounds; (2) to avoid a spillover of the war into China or the Soviet Union (the spillover into China prior to her entry into the war probably did not have a major impact on Chinese policy, but the incursion did create propaganda and political difficulties); (3) to avoid damaging, in the case of the hydroelectric plants, targets considered vital to the Chinese so as to avoid their entrance into the war, presumably in retaliation.

The Communists exercised far greater restraint on their air forces. Except for a few night "heckling" attacks from small biplanes in the spring of 1951 [85, p. 280] no air attacks were made on any targets in South Korea [199, p. 751]. The Communist restraint was not the result of the absence of inviting military targets. The port of Pusan was an extremely inviting target for bombardment and mining. It was the key to the American logistic effort and frequently was lighted up all night. American logistic convoys and troops in the field also could have been hampered by air attacks. A number of factors seem to have influenced the Communist decision not to respond in kind to United Nations air attacks on North Korea:

1. The Communists might have believed that it would have been very difficult, if not impossible, for the United Nations to continue its operations in Korea if Pusan came under heavy attack, and that, once the United Nations committed itself to the defense of South Korea, it was no longer in a position to accept complete withdrawal. Therefore, if attacks on logistic lines made impossible the continued conduct of an effective ground war in Korea, the United States might have been forced to engage in strategic strikes against the Chinese, if not the Russian, homeland.* If the Communists found this supposition credible, they may have concluded that, once their initial grab for South Korea failed, they could not afford to do anything that would lead to their complete control over South Korea.† They may have recognized that American confinement of the war to the Korean peninsula was dependent on her ability to fight there effectively.

2. In order to avoid attacks on Chinese air bases just north of the Yalu, Red airmen were not allowed to attack United Nations positions from these bases. Although the Communists were permitting the United States the sanctuary of bases in Japan and on aircraft carriers, they apparently were afraid that they would not be granted a similar sanctuary for bombing operations. United States planes managed to keep the North Korean airfields out of commission almost continuously throughout the war. Thus, given that the Chinese limited the use of their fields to staging operations and to fighter planes, the Communists were incapable of bombing operations [85, pp. 278, 637–638].

3. There is some evidence to suggest that Soviet pilots constituted a significant part of the "Chinese" air force during the Korean War [85, pp. 370, 651–652]. If this is true the explanation for target restraint

---

* The United States had secured British concurrence to bomb bases in China in the event of heavy air attacks from Chinese bases on United Nations troops (*H. C. Debs.*, 5th Series, CDXCVI, 970, Feb. 26, 1952) and this was probably communicated to the Chinese. However Truman reported that he was convinced that Russia would come in if Manchurian bases were bombed [310].

† This thesis implies that the Chinese would not have driven the United Nations forces off the Korean peninsula by ground action even if they had the capability. There is no evidence to substantiate or invalidate this point.

may have been the desire to avoid the capture of Soviet airmen. This proof of direct Soviet involvement in the war would at the least have been politically damaging and, from a Soviet point of view, might have created an intolerable risk of American retaliation.

By the end of the war the United States was exercising almost no target restraint in North Korea and the Communists were doing no bombing in South Korea. Each side was guided by a complex series of motives and incentives. However, despite the asymmetry of the actions, there is nothing to suggest that either side treated its decisions on targeting as being closely related to, affected by, or likely to affect, the opponent's decisions on these questions.

## EXPANSION AND LIMITATION

Decisions on expanding the United Nations operations resulted from the rejecting or approving of the field commanders' proposals by the Joint Chiefs of Staff or civilian officials. In some cases, particularly on the question of using atomic weapons, the military never made the request, and so, in some sense, no decision was made. On three occasions General MacArthur was refused his requests: to employ Chinese Nationalist troops, to impose a naval blockade on China, and to bomb bases and supply lines in China [199, p. 13]. But a number of MacArthur's requests for permission to expand the war were approved. These included the commitment of American ground forces, the Inchon offensive, and the crossing of the thirty-eighth parallel.

President Truman states that the National Security Council recommended the consideration of three factors relevant to the decision of whether to go on the offensive: action by the Soviet Union and the Chinese Communists, the views of friendly members of the United Nations, and the risk of general war [310, p. 359]. These and other decisions were also influenced by American doctrine as well as by domestic political pressures. The balancing of the factors varied from decision to decision, but all played a role in the major decisions to limit or expand the war.

Much less is known about the Communist decision-making process or the factors which influenced their decisions to limit or expand the war. The initial decision to keep the Chinese out of the war seems to have been based largely on domestic conditions in China, particularly the desire of the Chinese to implement their program of economic growth and development, and their desire to avoid military entanglements at a time when they had not yet consolidated their hold over their own country.* The reasons for the Russians' abstention from open intervention in the war are less clear. The Soviets were determined not to do anything that directly labeled them as participants; they did not publicize the participation of any Russian "volunteers" in the war, nor provide any atomic capability, although they did supply large amounts of conventional military equipment. One likely explanation is the Russian fear that intervention would lead to general war. The United States had the capability of inflicting great destruction on the Soviet homeland with its stock of atomic weapons, while the Soviets had no capability of directly attacking the United States, although they might have been able to capture a large part of Western Europe with ground forces. Thus the Soviets, aware of their inferior strategic position, were probably determined to keep out of the war and to provide no excuse for a direct American attack on the Soviet Union.

Each side apparently made its decisions to limit the war for different reasons and with minimal attention to the battlefield interaction. In addition the two sides observed very different limits. What the United States did in North Korea was quite different from what the Communists did in South Korea, but the Chinese used a much greater percentage of their gross national product than the United States did. Nevertheless, while the United States used naval vessels and airplanes to bomb troops and airfields within Korea, the Communists did not. The United States engaged in logistical interdiction; the Communists did not. Each side, then, observed its own series of limits and restraints only in some very general way related to, and dependent on, the limits of the other side.

At least a few of the limits were symmetrical. Both sides restricted their military operations almost entirely to Korea, and neither used nuclear weapons. There was lack of symmetry in that all the military targets in North Korea were attacked but most in South Korea were not. The United States attacked the Chinese points of entry—the Yalu bridges; but the Chinese did not attack the United States' points of entry—the ports. Both sides observed a number of what Schelling has called "legalistic" limitations [259, p. 1]. The United Nations carefully observed both the Chinese and Russian borders and tried to avoid crossing them inadvertently. There was symmetry in the absence of official declarations of war. The United Nations troops participated in the war in a "police action" capacity, and none of the countries involved, in-

---

* It was probably based also on the belief that the United States would not intervene and that the North Korean army would capture all of South Korea [329, pp. 40, 45–46]. The reasons for the Chinese entrance into the war were discussed earlier.

cluding the United States, declared war. The Chinese used "volunteers," and the Russians supplied equipment and presumably technicians, but little manpower for the battle.

In some cases the limits represented a recognition of the battlefield interaction. But the origin of many of the limits observed, and part of the explanation for others, lay not within the dynamics of the war itself, but within the domestic and international context in which the war was fought.

# 4

# Nuclear Weapons and Local War

PERHAPS THE MOST important thing to note about nuclear war is that one has never been fought. In contradistinction to conventional ground war of which there are numerous historical instances, troops have never used tactical nuclear weapons against each other on the battlefield. Thus no one really knows what tactical nuclear war would be like. One can envision several possibilities. The use of tactical nuclear weapons might as Schelling has suggested be mainly a symbolic act [265]. That is, one side might use tactical nuclear weapons as a device to increase substantially the shared risk that the war would become central either by expansion or explosion. The country would be using tactical nuclear weapons not because of their likely influence on the battlefield but as a symbolic act, and would therefore be concerned to use them to demonstrate its own seriousness—to demonstrate the danger that the war might get out of hand—rather than to affect the outcome of the battlefield war. In this case the response of the enemy might well be on the same level, either a backing down on the basis of this demonstration of seriousness, or a corresponding use of tactical nuclear weapons in an effort to force the enemy to desist. Even in this case both sides are likely to remain concerned with the tactical outcome of the war, as well as with the maneuvering to show seriousness, but they will be much less concerned than they would be if tactical nuclear weapons were used with other purposes in mind. However, even if nuclear weapons are used specifically for the purpose of altering the battlefield tactical war, they will still increase the shared risk of central war.

There is also the possibility that relatively large (two kilotons or larger) nuclear weapons would be used as part of a tactical ground war. In this case it may be that the nuclear weapons would be dropped from planes or from short-range missiles and would not necessarily be carried by the troops in the field. Such use of tactical nuclear weapons is likely to alter ground war in ways that are by no means easy to predict.* Finally, very small tactical nuclear weapons (below one kiloton) might be used as part of a ground war that looked very much like conventional warfare. Such nuclear weapons would not be significantly larger (and in some cases would be much smaller) than high-explosive weapons. They would be physically smaller and would carry more explosive power per man and per pound than do high explosives. Their use would be similar to any increase of approximately a factor of five in the efficiency of explosives [33, p. 254]. If (as seems doubtful) a nuclear war could be fought with only these very small nuclear weapons, then the battle might be very much like that of conventional warfare. This type of nuclear war is discussed by B. H. Liddell-Hart [181, pp. 74–81], who concludes that it would not be to the military advantage of the West on the battlefield.

## DEVELOPMENT OF THE DEBATE †

The first efforts to analyze the possible role of tactical nuclear weapons in ground warfare were carried on within the American government beginning in 1948. Project Vista at the California Institute of Technology was an effort to discover to what uses tactical nuclear weapons could be put. The situation considered was implicitly (if not explicitly) that of local warfare. As a result of Project Vista the United States began to take seriously the potential of the uses of tactical nuclear weapons; and a process began which was ultimately to see tactical nuclear weapons become standard equipment for American military forces.

In 1952 the United States tested its first thermonuclear device, as did the Soviet Union a few months later. Within a short time, fusion bombs of vastly greater power than fission weapons were available on both

---

* In this image it is generally assumed that troops will be dispersed and that the war will resemble guerrilla warfare. This has been the official Army view. [See, for example, House Subcommittee of the Committee on Appropriations Hearings, *Department of Defense Appropriations for 1961*, Part 2, pp. 411 and 433]. It is also the image implied by Kissinger [159].

† For a general discussion of the development of local-war doctrine, see Halperin [106].

sides. This development was important in two ways in assessing the role of nuclear weapons in local war. It increased very substantially the physical cost of a central war and hence the importance of preventing the explosion of a local war. The development also raised the possibility that very large (megaton) weapons would be used tactically on the battlefield. Such action would alter completely the character of ground warfare in a way that has yet to be explored. Nearly all analysts in this field have ignored this development, failing to distinguish between the destructive power of fission and fusion weapons.

The Army announced in 1953 that it was experimenting to discover the effect that nuclear weapons would have on infantry combat. In the same year two army officers, William Kintner and George Reinhardt, published a book-length, technical study of the uses of nuclear weapons in land combat [155]. The first mention of the possible tactical uses of nuclear weapons in the general literature appeared at the same time in Ralph Lapp's somewhat technical study of the implications of nuclear weapons [170]. At that time Lapp assumed that nuclear weapons were relatively scarce but that they would be used in a local war. The scarcity argument dropped out of the debate almost before it got in, however, and it has been generally assumed from that point on that nuclear weapons are in fact cheaper per unit of fire power than conventional explosives, and as plentiful.

In January of 1954 Brodie published an article in which he explored the uses of nuclear weapons as a tactical tool, that is, as suitable for use against battlefield targets. His primary concern was with general war; but, toward the end of the article, he alluded to local war and expressed the belief that nuclear weapons would have to be used, at least in Europe, to compensate for the Communist manpower advantage [35]. In November of 1954 Frank Sackton published in a military journal an article in which he explored the battlefield uses of nuclear weapons and concluded that the West would always gain from their use because of its technological superiority [253].

The NATO Council committed itself in late 1954 to the use of tactical nuclear weapons in the defense of Europe but continued to rule out the possibility of local warfare on the European continent.* In January of 1955 Richard Leghorn in an article in *U. S. News & World Report* urged the West to adopt a nuclear strategy to overcome the Communist manpower advantage. He suggested that the West should use tactical nuclear weapons to meet a Communist conventional ground attack and should threaten strategic counterforce in the event that the Soviets should seek to use nuclear weapons tactically [173].

* For a discussion of the evolution of NATO doctrine on the use of nuclear weapons, see Osgood [228, pp. 102–171].

In February of 1955 Thomas Phillips warned that American forces would soon be equipped only to fight with nuclear weapons and that "then the stage will be reached when war will be only atomic and total" [233, p. 8]. In October of the same year Brodie published an article in *Harper's Magazine* in which he restated his belief that the use of tactical nuclear weapons would make up for Western numerical inferiority on the Europeon continent [37].

The years 1956–1958 saw a great deal of writing on the use of nuclear weapons. Arthur Hadley published an article in *The Reporter* of April 19, 1956 in which he proposed a highly mobile brigade—equipped with small tactical nuclear weapons—which would fly around the world putting out brush fires started by the enemy [100]. There were a number of assumptions here, including the image of an enemy equipped only with conventional weapons or with inferior tactical nuclear weapons, which were soon to be outdistanced by the facts.

At the same time study groups on the problems of nuclear warfare were meeting both at the Council on Foreign Relations in New York and at Chatham House in England. In April of 1956 preliminary reports of the deliberations of the two groups were published in their journals. Henry Kissinger in *Foreign Affairs* [158] presented in abbreviated form the case for using nuclear weapons in local war, which was to be elaborated in his book. Anthony Buzzard in *International Affairs* [49] (and in *World Politics* [48]) sketched the Chatham House doctrine of graduated deterrence. This was a policy which called for developing a series of possible responses depending on the nature of the Communist military attack and in addition called for the use of nuclear weapons in large local wars.

Toward the end of 1956 the United States Army announced that it had activated its first division capable of fighting with nuclear weapons. At the same time a book appeared and an article was being written which were to question seriously for the first time the advantage to the United States of using tactical nuclear weapons.

The book, a collection of essays which dealt with general aspects of military policy was edited by William Kaufmann and written by members of the Princeton Center of International Studies [143]. The essays questioned previous assumptions. Kaufmann [142] pointed out that many writers had assumed an American monopoly of nuclear power. Once one concedes parity of nuclear power, he wrote, then the United States may not gain from the use of atomic weapons; and, in any case, it is impossible to make a decision except in concrete situations.

In January of 1957 *Foreign Affairs* published the first journal article devoted to a detailed consideration of the problems of using nuclear weapons in local war. The burden of James King's argument in the article was that the United States should not initiate the use of nuclear weapons. He suggested that given nuclear parity, tactical nuclear weapons are not clearly to the advantage of the United States. He stressed the difficulties in keeping a nuclear war limited and the political costs of initiating the use of nuclear weapons. In addition, he cited the article by Kissinger [159] which has been discussed, indicating his opposition to it [149].

In the following month Brodie published another article which indicated the direction in which his thought was moving. He too cited the difficulties in keeping a nuclear war limited, though he asserted that "this is not to say that we may not use nuclear weapons in local war; it only underlines the problem of finding out how we can use them without thereby signaling the abandonment of restraints" [39, p. 60].

Later in 1957 two books on local war precipitated a major debate on the problems of using nuclear weapons. The first, Osgood's, presented a balanced discussion of the role of nuclear weapons [223]. Kissinger, however, presented an argument for the use of nuclear weapons in local war. He began his discussion of the problem by summarizing King's arguments against using nuclear weapons, and proceeded to a presentation of his own views without dealing specifically with King's points [159].

In reviews of Kissinger's book national-security experts were generally alike in praising its discussion of military policy in general and its critique of United States policy, but attacking the study because of the proposals on nuclear war. King wrote his review [150] in two parts; the first praised the book, the second one reiterated his position on tactical nuclear weapons and discussed the points raised in Kissinger's book. Paul Nitze's review [216] was more generally critical and indicated that he too had retreated from his previous support for the use of nuclear weapons. Kaufmann's review [146] was the most critical, pointing out numerous inconsistencies in Kissinger's analysis and bearing down heavily on the scheme for nuclear war. Reviewing three books on limited war, Brodie meanwhile had revealed that he now rejected the notion that the United States would gain a military advantage from the use of nuclear weapons. He stressed the problems of keeping a nuclear war limited [40].

By the end of 1958 the discussion seemed to have run out of new arguments. The analysts who had been associated with the British Chatham House group had stopped talking about graduated deterrence and had begun to suggest that perhaps the West would be better off if nuclear weapons were not used. Brodie published a book making clear his conversion [42].

Very little was added to the public dialogue until 1960, when Kissinger in an article titled "Limited War: Nuclear or Conventional?— A Reappraisal," indicated a substantial revision in his thinking about the use of nuclear weapons. Citing three factors: (1) the disagreement within the American military establishment about the nature of nuclear local war; (2) the growth of the Soviet nuclear stockpile and the increased significance of long-range missiles; and (3) the impact of arms-control negotiations, Kissinger concluded that the conventional capability of the free world should be such a size that a nuclear defense "becomes the *last* and not the *only* recourse" [163, p. 146 (italics in the original)].

The debate, however, was not over. In the same volume in which Kissinger's article appeared, Edward Teller argued that the use of tactical nuclear weapons was to the advantage of the United States. He urged the further testing of nuclear weapons to improve America's tactical arsenal [304]. In 1959 Oskar Morgenstern had published a study which devoted a chapter to limited war and repeated all of the arguments for using nuclear weapons [201]. And in 1960 Thomas Murray, a former member of the Atomic Energy Commission, had urged the adoption of a nuclear-war strategy and called for the United States to develop an arsenal of "tens of thousands" of small tactical weapons. He again repeated the arguments which had been used in 1957 and 1958 for their use [209]. In 1962 Teller published a book in which he reiterated the arguments for the use of nuclear weapons [305].

At the policy level the notion that the West would gain a strategic advantage by using tactical nuclear weapons and hence should rely primarily on the nuclear capability is in the process of being reversed by the Kennedy administration. President Kennedy entered office committed to strengthening American conventional forces and brought with him a number of students of military strategy committed to developing a substantial conventional capability. American military planning which had assumed that tactical nuclear weapons will be used in anything but a very small war has begun to change. Even NATO strategy which has rested explicitly on the intention to use nuclear weapons in any show of force seems to be changing on the basis of the kind of reasoning to be explored in this chapter.

## THE RISK OF CENTRAL WAR

The question of the extent to which the use of nuclear weapons increases the likelihood that a local war explodes or expands drastically has provoked considerable dispute. Those advocating the use of nuclear weapons have tried to prove that the use of nuclear weapons is not likely to cause central war. There is much uncertainty on this question; the weight of the available analysis, however, suggests that nuclear war is considerably more likely to explode than is conventional war.

Other boundary conditions are stressed by those advocating the use of tactical nuclear weapons. Buzzard suggested that in any case the most important limit would be in targets, not weapons. He equated "tactical" and "strategic" with targets "acceptable" and "unacceptable" in a local war [49, p. 148]. Teller [304] and others have been prepared to give up the weapons limitation on the grounds that this limit is not a crucial one, and that a war could be kept limited if other restraints are observed, particularly those of objectives and targets. There is a certain ambiguity here. It is not always clear if the argument is that one can never establish an effective weapons limit or simply that the advantages to be gained from using nuclear weapons make it worthwhile to remove this restraint.

The use of nuclear weapons in a local war would, as Nitze has suggested, make much more difficult the maintaining of target limitations [218, p. 60]. Air bases are perhaps the most crucial instance. It is likely that the enemy would bomb air bases from which planes were leaving to attack troops and installations with tactical nuclear weapons. Manchuria and Japan might well become targets in a future Korean war, for example, if the planes using these sanctuaries dropped highly destructive tactical nuclear weapons. The Army's war-game experiences, Operations Carte Blanche and Sage Brush, revealed this pattern of target expansion brought about by the use of nuclear weapons [18, p. 40]. The use of tactical nuclear weapons would increase pressures to bomb enemy sanctuaries.

As was suggested at the beginning of the chapter, both sides understand conventional warfare, they know that it can be controlled in the present age, but neither understands what nuclear warfare is or whether or not it can be restrained. The first time that nuclear weapons were used both sides would feel that an important new dimension had been introduced into the war. Neither would be clear as to what its implications were. Both sides would probably ask themselves whether this meant that central war, either immediately or in the short run, had become inevitable. In this way the use of tactical nuclear weapons in a local war would probably substantially increase the pressures towards preemption and might set off a spiral of preemptive expectations which would lead to explosion. In addition, the use of nuclear weapons in a local war would break one of the most important barriers to the expansion of a local war. Thus, while the introduction of nuclear weapons would not make central war inevitable, it would substantially increase the risk of central war. The optimum strategy for either or both sides in a local war is not necessarily to do whatever limits the war. There may be situations in which the United States would want to introduce tactical nuclear weapons precisely because they increase the risk of central war, but the government should recognize that this is the implication of the introduction of nuclear weapons.

## COSTS AND GAINS

In determining policy on the use of tactical nuclear weapons in a local war, each side will consider not only the danger of explosion but also what the political and battlefield costs and gains would be.

### Battlefield Advantage

The main argument used by advocates of the use of nuclear weapons in local war is that the United States would gain a battlefield advantage over its Communist opponent by their use. The major hypotheses which have been advanced to prove this proposition are that nuclear weapons permit the substitution of technology for manpower, that nuclear weapons are more valuable to the defense than to the offense, and that the United States can develop a superior arsenal for fighting nuclear war.

Probably the most frequently made assertion (for example, by Murray [209, p. 65]) about tactical nuclear weapons is that they permit the substitution of technology for manpower, by inter alia preventing the massing of large numbers of troops. The assumption is that the Communists have a significant manpower advantage over the West. Certainly in Europe this is not the case: the NATO population is greater than that of the Soviet Union and its satellites. Even in Asia the West may not be doomed to a manpower disadvantage. A smaller number of troops, it is argued, have an advantage in the use of weapons with great fire power. Why this would be an advantage is not clear, unless the unstated assumption is that the enemy is not using tactical nuclear weapons or for some reason is using them in a highly inefficient way.

P. M. S. Blackett [27, p. 784], King [150, p. 17], and others have argued that the minimum number of troops to hold an area will not be reduced if both sides use nuclear weapons, and the number might in fact increase. Some Army war games indicate that troop casualties will be much higher in nuclear war. High attrition rates will help the side with the larger number of reserves, not the reverse, and while it is true that the individual unit will have a smaller number of men, this does not mean that the number of units will not be crucial.

The upper limit of manpower that can be used on a battlefield of a fixed size is likely to be lower in a nuclear war. But until and unless this limit is reached, and given the possibility of a geographic expansion of the war and the need for troop reserves, numbers will be as important in nuclear as in nonnuclear war. The argument that the use of nuclear weapons brings a strategic asymmetry in favor of the smaller force does not stand the test of analysis—nor does the proposition advanced by Teller [304] and others that nuclear weapons bring a strategic asymmetry in favor of the defensive side. In order to prove that the use of nuclear weapons is to the advantage of the United States on this point, one would have to show first the strategic asymmetry and second that the United States is in fact more likely to be on the defensive.

Teller [304] asserts that an offensive action requires the massing of troops, which provides an excellent target for tactical nuclear weapons, and that small mobile units (which would be used in tactical nuclear war) are effective in depriving the enemy of territory. Here again the unstated assumption seems to be that the enemy does not have tactical nuclear weapons or at least that his weapons are not mobile. Once one concedes to both sides small mobile forces equipped with tactical nuclear weapons, the advantage is not necessarily with the defensive. While there will be problems in massing for attack, there will be similar problems of holding a defensive position.

In conventional ground warfare it is generally accepted that the defensive has a substantial advantage over the offensive. As much as a three-to-one advantage may be required for an offensive force to be successful [181]. With the use of tactical nuclear weapons it seems likely that this advantage for the defensive will be erased. In a tactical nuclear war the defensive and offensive are at least on an equal plane, or perhaps, as Albert Wohlstetter has suggested, the use of tactical nuclear weapons may give a decisive advantage to the offensive [335, pp. 33–34]. The use of tactical nuclear weapons might make it possible for the attacking side to eliminate the existing forces of the defender, reach his immediate tactical objective, and end the war before the defending side can mobilize more forces. Tactical nuclear war may well put a premium on surprise and forces-in-being which would aid the aggressive attacker rather than the defender.

Even if nuclear weapons aided the defensive side it would have to be noted that the United States may not be more often on the defensive. Assuming that a local war may very well begin with a major Communist offensive, for most of the war the United States will be on the offensive seeking to restore the *status quo* by recovering lost ground. (This was, of course, the pattern in Korea.) Certainly this is not the only possible course for a ground war, but there is no reason to assume a priori that the United States would gain from a technological innovation which aids the defensive.

An additional strategic asymmetry, it is argued, is that the United States' superiority in industrial potential and broad range of technology gives the West an advantage in nuclear war. In the arguments discussed up to now, the introduction of nuclear weapons has been seen to have an uncertain effect. However, in terms of industrial potential and logistics (which will be discussed next), use of nuclear weapons would bring about a strategic *disadvantage* to the United States.

It is argued that the United States because of its greater industrial potential and technological ability could develop better tactical nuclear weapons than the enemy. It is not made clear why the United States could develop better tactical nuclear weapons but not better conventional weapons. King in fact suggests that the emphasis on nuclear weapons, "to the degree that it enables the Communists to concentrate their scarce resources in a limited area of production, appears to be tantamount to abandoning just that much of the advantage given to the United States by general productive superiority" [149, p. 252]. In fact the United States is now faced with approximate Communist parity in nuclear weapons. But, as discussed hereafter, in the broader area of conventional weapons technology, the United States might find it possible to develop a decided advantage.

In the field of logistics the Western advantage in not using nuclear weapons is even clearer. There is general agreement that the United States is more likely to be faced with logistics problems than is its opponent. The enemy will probably have interior lines of supply while the United States supply line is likely to be longer and to require movements by ship. American supply lines will be more susceptible to attack. Ports, in particular, are an easy target for bombing and are likely to be an important link in the American logistics chain.

But both Morgenstern [201, p. 142] and Kissinger [159, p. 180] argued that logistics problems will be minor in nuclear war. This position is based on the assumption of the development of a technology which does not exist and on a failure to think through some infantry problems. Kissinger argued that the United States must develop a completely self-sufficient military unit. He then proceeded to assume that such units exist and based his argument on this. Given such units, logistics is clearly not a problem. However the technical problems involved include the need to develop a solid fuel for tanks and other vehicles of mobility and the existence of weapons which do not break down or require numerous spare parts. Finally, the proposition assumes that the units also will not need conventional fire power.

But, as King [150, p. 17] has pointed out, a unit equipped with nuclear weapons would have to be guarded with conventional weapons large enough to defeat any force which was too small to use nuclear weapons against. Unless a force had conventional weapons it could not defend itself against guerrilla attacks designed to overcome the nuclear unit. The logistics problem might be quantitatively easier since nuclear forces would require smaller amounts of supplies. In some cases it might be possible to drop these by air. Logistics, however, will remain a problem even in nuclear war, and the use of tactical nuclear weapons will only increase the difficulty of keeping open the long American supply routes.

In some cases the use of tactical nuclear weapons might help the United States overcome its logistic disadvantage. If the use of tactical nuclear weapons could be restricted to the very low range (below one kiloton), it would substantially alleviate the logistics problem since a much smaller quantity of supplies would be needed to deliver a given amount of fire power. However the use of such small tactical nuclear weapons would not substantially improve the ability of the enemy to take out American logistic lines, particularly ports. This suggests that the United States, from the point of view of logistics, would gain from the use of very small tactical nuclear weapons, but for this very reason it may be impossible to limit the use of tactical nuclear weapons to these very small weapons. That is, the use of such weapons may be sufficient for the purposes of the United States and not the enemy, and, in view of the lack of any clear division between very small and somewhat larger tactical nuclear weapons, it is likely that the enemy would expand the war to the use of larger weapons.

Thus a consideration of the strategic asymmetries of nuclear weapons indicates first that the asymmetries are not as great as suggested by some writers; second, that it is not always clear who would gain from the asymmetries; and third, that at least in terms of the logistics and industrial capacity the Communists seem more likely to gain. The question of who would gain from the use of tactical nuclear weapons can only be answered by saying that it depends on a host of variables including who uses them first, the geographic area, the terrain, the sympathies of the indigenous population, and the state of technology and production at the time.

## Deterrence

Is the threat of using nuclear weapons a more effective deterrent to the initiating of local war than the threat of fighting conventionally? Or is an ambiguous policy most effective?

The threat of using nuclear weapons might pose a less credible threat if the Communists believed that the United States would be less likely to intervene if doing so meant that they would thereby initiate the use of nuclear weapons. There are many parts of the world, however, where American intervention against an overt attack would be automatic. In the NATO area, Japan, the Philippines, and Taiwan, the United States commitment to defend the area is such that the Communists are not likely to doubt that the United States will intervene. In such areas the threat of using nuclear weapons is likely to be a more effective deterrent of local war. However an American threat to use nuclear weapons might serve to deter the United States from taking a strong stand itself in ambiguous situations such as a Soviet squeeze in Berlin.

As was suggested earlier one of the purposes of fighting a local war is to increase the shared risk of central war. Thus, the threat to use nuclear weapons is more effective partly because it increases the prospective cost of military aggression, but more importantly because the threat increases the risk that aggression will lead to explosion. The threat to use nuclear weapons constitutes a declared willingness to increase the shared risk that central war will develop even though neither side wants it. By making the threat the United States also indicates the importance it gives to defending the country in question.

However, in areas where the United States decision to intervene in a local war will not be automatic, the effect of a decision to rely on nuclear weapons is more questionable, and might very well reduce the credibility of the American local-war deterrent. The willingness to intervene (and Communist recognition of this intention) is much more important as a deterrent than the manner of intervention.

## Battlefield "Cost"

The frequently made assertion that a nuclear war will "cost" less for the West has been used to mean a number of different things. The cost of delivering explosive power will, in fact, be significantly cheaper if nuclear weapons are used. This can be most graphically illustrated in terms of the saturation level for a given target, that is, the force needed to completely destroy a target. Except for very small targets (for example, a few infantrymen) the munitions and delivery system needed to saturate a target will be much cheaper to produce if nuclear weapons are used. In a conventional war the industrial base will be crucial both because of the higher cost of saturation (and lower levels of destruction) and because the war is likely to last longer. In a nuclear war, because saturation is cheap and because the war is likely to be short, the vastly superior American industrial potential will not weigh in the balance.

Not more than a few thousand nuclear weapons could be profitably employed in a local war. (That many in the kiloton range or above would destroy most of Western Europe.) On the other hand, the number of conventional weapons that might be used runs to at least several hundred thousand. The number of delivery systems that could be used in a conventional environment would be scaled similarly. The amount of matériel needed to saturate a target is vastly greater in a conventional attack—so much larger that very few (if any) conventional battles have ever been fought at the saturation level. This means that the marginal utility of increments of materiel is much greater for conventional warfare. This is the resource in which the United States is the richest nation in the world. Therefore, to the extent that the expense of a war in terms of resources can be increased, the United States gains a strategic advantage.

Blackett [27, p. 784], King [150, p. 16], and others have argued that the use of nuclear weapons must involve great costs, in that their use would lead to the large-scale destruction of civilian populations. Clearly this depends on where the war is fought. However, if one considers present technology and the destructive power of nuclear weapons, there will be extensive damage to civilian populations and cities in almost any area of the world. Most airfields are situated near cities. Armies use roads, railroads, and bridges, all closely connected with civilian populations. The use of a few thousand tactical weapons in the kiloton range (certainly conceivable in a ground war) would result in the devastation of several thousand square miles and possibly in many millions of civilian casualties. Thus extensive civilian damage might be impossible to avoid even if both sides attempted to do so.

Troop casualties may well be higher if nuclear weapons are used. Although units would be smaller, more troops might be placed in the field. In addition casualties per unit are likely to be very high because of the destructive power of nuclear weapons and the effects of fallout from even very low-yield weapons. Even with any possible degree of dispersion, a total of 2000 tactical nuclear weapons of a few kilotons' yield is sufficient to destroy completely a very large field army of 25 line divisions. In practice a much smaller number would probably suffice.

## Political Costs and Gains

The political costs of initiating the use of nuclear weapons tend to be ignored by the advocators. Morgenstern simply states that the world aversion to the use of nuclear weapons comes from progapanda which is "unmitigated nonsense" [201, p. 153]. Kissinger [159] implied throughout his study that since nuclear war is the only viable military policy, the United States must be prepared to suffer the political costs involved, and he suggested as did Osgood [223, p. 257], that an effective propaganda campaign could substantially reduce the political costs of using nuclear weapons.

Those who argue that conventional local war is also a viable military strategy have examined the political costs of initiating the use of nuclear weapons and have found them to be very substantial. The general opposition of many people to the use of nuclear weapons, the feeling that somehow they are different and immoral, would bring about great shock and disillusionment on the part of neutrals, allies, and Americans themselves if nuclear weapons were used. In addition states are likely to be less eager to accept American military aid if the United States intends to use tactical nuclear weapons in defending them. The damage which would be done to any country by the use of tactical nuclear weapons may lead many states to seek neutrality and to prefer surrender to defense by the United States. Some countries, including West Germany, however, which have emphasized deterrence rather than defense, have sought a guarantee that nuclear weapons would be used in their defense.

The use of nuclear weapons in a local war by either the United States or the Soviet Union might substantially speed up the process of the diffusion of nuclear weapons to Nth countries. Certainly, if one of the reasons that a number of countries have not made the decision to develop nuclear weapons is, as Kahn [136] has argued, the feeling that somehow these weapons are not used in wars, then their use in a local war would have strong effects leading to the diffusion of nuclear weapons.

The American threat to use nuclear weapons in the defense of third areas has been reassuring to our allies to some extent. In particular the

American commitment to use nuclear weapons in the defense of Europe has contributed to the strength of the NATO alliance and the faith which America's allies have had in its willingness to come to their defense in the event of a military attack. Should the United States formally renounce the use of nuclear weapons in the defense of third areas, this might have serious short-run repercussions until the United States made it clear that it expected to use other means to deal effectively with the threat of Communist military action.

However the political costs are likely to be great if the United States should initiate the use of nuclear weapons. A propaganda campaign stressing the "conventional" nature of tactical nuclear weapons might soften the blow but could not eliminate it.

## AMERICAN POLICY

This analysis of what nuclear local war might be like suggests a number of implications for American military policy in terms of the capability for conventional and nuclear local war which the United States should have, what the United States should want the Soviets to believe about how it might use this capability, and how the United States should in fact use it.

Despite the wide disagreements discussed, the capabilities problem has not caused much controversy. Almost all writers have seen the need for both a nuclear and a conventional war capability.* Morgenstern takes perhaps the most extreme position, arguing the need for a conventional force only large enough to cope with riots and other military actions *short* of guerrilla warfare [201]. There is wide agreement, however, that situations might arise in which the United States would not want to initiate the use of nuclear weapons, and also that the United States must be able to use tactical nuclear weapons even if only in response to Russian use.

The Army and many analysts have suggested "dual-purpose" forces as the "ideal" solution. There are major problems, however, in actually sending a force into combat equipped to fight both conventionally and with nuclear weapons. If such a force were supplied with nuclear weapons, it might ultimately use them under the strains of the battle without authority to do so. Two alternatives are possible. One is to have stand-by forces equipped with nuclear weapons should the United States engage in a conventional limited war; the other is to plan on

---

* The size of the forces needed for conventional and nuclear limited wars has caused considerable controversy, however.

restricting the use of nuclear weapons to supporting units outside the battlefield area, that is, by tactical air forces and by short-range or longer-range missiles. The major problem in such use is that it may lead to an expansion of the war into areas from which the nuclear weapons are coming. This problem might be overcome in part by flying planes carrying nuclear weapons from aircraft carriers. The United States has adopted the policy of seeking to equip American troops to fight both with and without tactical nuclear weapons—and this seems to be the worst alternative. Which of these three policies is, in fact, most desirable requires far more detailed analysis than can be given here. In any case the point remains that the United States must maintain a capability to fight either conventionally or with tactical nuclear weapons and must be prepared to shift courses quickly in a local war.

## Communication of Intentions

If we assume that the United States should proceed with a revised dual-capability policy, what are the implications for communication policy? Three basic policies have been suggested.

The first is that the United States threaten to initiate the use of tactical nuclear weapons in certain specified conditions, in particular if NATO (or presumably any other friendly force) is about to be over-run in a conventional war. The second policy that has been proposed is for the United States to state it will never initiate the use of nuclear weapons. The third is for the United States to communicate that it might use nuclear weapons but not to specify under what conditions.

A firm declaration not to initiate the use of nuclear weapons involves certain gains as well as some serious costs. If one is worried that the Russians might use nuclear weapons because they anticipate that the United States will use them first, then there is much to be said for such a declaration. It will also give impetus to the drive to strengthen American and alliance conventional forces and contribute to retarding the spread of nuclear weapons. By increasing the expectation that a local war would remain conventional, a no-first-use declaration might permit the United States to be more willing to run the risk of local war in defending its interests.

On the other hand, such a commitment might make the deterrent less effective and might give the enemy certain tactical advantages in conventional warfare. If the Russians became convinced that the United States would not initiate the use of nuclear weapons even if presented with very inviting targets, then they might be more prone to risk a war and might take greater chances in massing men in larger numbers for longer periods during a local war. In the short run, an expressed American reluctance to use nuclear weapons to repel a conventional attack might stimulate the proliferation of nuclear weapons among the United States' NATO allies. The current American policy of expressing a willingness to use nuclear weapons if necessary is aimed partly at convincing the Europeans that they do not need independent nuclear capabilities. The policy may also reflect a continuing belief that the introduction of tactical nuclear weapons will improve NATO's tactical position.

Despite the costs, American policy should be aimed at reinforcing the difference between nuclear and conventional weapons. The United States should stress its emphasis on conventional forces and its feeling that they are more effective than tactical nuclear forces in the defense of local areas. If the American government can convince its allies that the action does not signify a reduced determination to defend them, the United States should renounce the first use of nuclear weapons.

## Action Policy

Finally, the action policy of the United States must be considered. Teller [305], Morgenstern [201], and others have suggested that the United States use tactical nuclear weapons in *any* local war. At the other extreme is the proposal that the United States use nuclear weapons only if the enemy uses them first. The previous analysis suggests that the proposal to use nuclear weapons in any local war stems from an underestimation of the danger of a nuclear war exploding and from an erroneous conception that the United States would inevitably gain from the use of nuclear weapons. The proposal that nuclear weapons be used if necessary to prevent a local defeat also reflects the view that the United States would gain from the introduction of nuclear weapons. But there are not likely to be many (if any) situations in which the introduction of nuclear weapons would improve the West's tactical situation and any use of nuclear weapons will result in many political costs to the United States as well as increasing the likelihood of an explosion.

It would seem, therefore, that in almost any conceivable local war the United States should not introduce nuclear weapons. But this should not be taken as absolute: there may be some situations in which the United States ought to initiate the use of tactical nuclear weapons. In any case the United States should be prepared to meet any conventional aggression without introducing nuclear weapons, and also to be able to fight at a nuclear level. The instances in which the United States should itself introduce nuclear weapons in a local war are likely to be rare, and the burden of proof should rest squarely on those advocating such first use. But the prospect cannot be ruled out entirely, and, since the Russians may introduce tactical nuclear weapons, the United States must maintain an effective dual capacity.

# 5

# Arms Control and Local War

M OST ARMS-CONTROL agreements which have been suggested either formally by the United States or the Soviet Union, or which have been discussed by military analysts, are aimed at reducing the likelihood of central war. Central war, much more than local war, may occur inadvertently, and both sides would stand to lose in most central wars relative to their prewar positions. The common interest in avoiding central war is clearly greater than any mutual interest in avoiding local wars.*

Any arms-control agreement, however, which affects the strategic balance also has an effect on local wars. The nature of the effect is by no means obvious and depends both on the nature of the agreement, and on the interest of both sides in maintaining the agreement. Nevertheless there are some general relationships between strategic arms control and local war.

Most arms-control agreements relating to central war would probably be concerned in one way or another with "stabilizing the strategic balance." They would attempt to reduce the likelihood of war's breaking out, either by premeditated action, preventive urges, or "accidents." In order to do this they are likely to move strategic forces in the direction of being capable of surviving a strategic attack and then retaliating. Such forces would not give rise to preemptive urges. In addition the danger of an accident's leading to war would be greatly reduced since both sides could take the time to discover whether or not the event was really an accident, or a signal that central war was about to start. Such

* For an extended discussion of the possible role of arms control in relation to central war, see Schelling and Halperin [264, pp. 9–23] and Halperin [105].

agreements might "make the world safe for local war." But the relationship is far too complex to admit of such a simple statement. There are pressures both ways which need to be explored. While this can be done in general terms, the actual determination of whether a particular agreement is likely to increase the probability of local war depends on the precise nature of the agreement as well as the general factors to be discussed.

To the extent that a major strategic arms-control agreement reassures the major powers against the outbreak of central war, the agreement will take some of the *risk* out of local war itself. As discussed previously, one of the main inhibitions on the initiation of local war at the present time (as well as an inhibition on the expansion of local war) is the fear that some event during the war will cause it to explode into central war. But if the urge to preempt is sufficiently calmed down, if false alarms or the responses to them are made less dangerous, and if the scale of destruction even in the event of central war is made to appear somewhat less cataclysmic than it otherwise might, one somewhat paradoxical result may be to make local war less risky.

Not only might strategic arms-control agreements reduce the danger from engaging in local war which comes from the danger of inadvertent strategic war, but they would also reduce substantially the credibility of the threat of a first strike. If both sides have collaborated in programs to make their own *and each other's* strategic forces reasonably indestructible under attack, neither could very credibly threaten deliberate initiation of central war in a case of local aggression. In addition an arms-control agreement relating to strategic forces, particularly one that included international inspection of such forces, would suggest that both sides would use the strategic forces only if the agreement were violated and the other side unleashed its strategic forces. Thus not only the credibility of massive retaliation but also the legitimacy of making massive retaliation threats would be jeopardized by a strategic-war agreement. Threats of limited retaliation against the major opponent would be similarly affected. Any attempt to pull out some forces to use them for limited retaliation might not only jeopardize the agreement, but would also suggest to the other side that the agreement was being broken for the purpose of initiating central war. This might touch off just the war that both sides were seeking to avoid.

In addition to altering the danger of strategic war in ways that make local war more likely, strategic arms control might more directly affect the incentives of various countries to initiate local war. Strategic arms control may freeze the existing balance of power in a way that prevents other countries from joining the nuclear-missile club, and this may create positive incentives for Nth countries to seek to break the agreement. Even if Communist China somehow was forced into an arms-control arrangement which prevented it from getting nuclear weapons and missiles, the Chinese government is not likely to be happy about such a situation. And while China might not be able to do anything directly to break the agreement, it might have a very great interest in creating conditions which force the Soviet Union or the United States to abrogate the agreement and agree to the spread of nuclear weapons and missiles. The easiest way to do this might be to raise tensions deliberately or use force in areas around the Chinese border, by reopening the Korean War, increasing supplies to Vietnamese rebels, or most likely by resuming the shelling of Quemoy or Matsu. The Chinese in this way might force the United States into breaking the existing strategic arms-control arrangements. Even if China (or for that matter, one of America's allies) does not deliberately create crises or local wars in an effort to force the breakdown of an arms-control arrangement, it may not be deterred from engaging in such actions simply because they might lead to the breakdown of the agreement. China and other powers are likely to lack the positive incentive to maintain the agreement that the Soviet Union and the United States would have.

In addition to third powers that might have a positive incentive to cause the breakdown of an arms-control agreement between the United States and the Soviet Union, there might be individuals and factions within the two countries that were interested in the breakdown, or at least in the secret violation of a strategic arms-control agreement. Such groups might view the stirring up of tension or international violence either as an excuse to abrogate the strategic arms-control agreement, or as a cover under which the agreement might be violated. All kinds of unusual activities would seem "justified" in a country that was busy with a local war; one expects unusual military communications, movement of military forces, intelligence activities, and so forth, to be a natural accompaniment of the domestic emergency that goes with external war. Thus the initiation of local war might be the cloak for large-scale evasion that had already been decided upon, or an attempt to create a favorable climate to get agreement within the government on evasion, or a means of creating pressures for the abrogation of the arms-control agreement. Factions interested in the breakdown of the agreement might be as successful in getting the other side to abrogate as their own government.

Thus there are a number of factors which suggest that strategic arms control might well increase the likelihood of local war. Even if these factors dominated, it might be a price worth paying. The United States might willingly accept a situation in which local wars were more likely if it could thereby reduce substantially the danger of central war. But such agreements should not be accepted without a clear understanding of the risks involved. However, there are some countervailing pressures which make it less obvious that strategic arms control would inevitably pave the way for more local wars.

It can be supposed that any substantial measure of nuclear disarmament would result only from some greater recognition than presently exists of the common interests that the United States shares with the Russians in the avoidance of war and the tranquilization of international violence. To assume major strategic arms control and to suppose that in every other respect the world is unchanged is unreasonable. Thus the sheer improved understanding on both sides of the need for restraint in military actions, and the improved ability of both sides to act on that understanding, is probably a prerequisite for an extensive disarmament and would itself undoubtedly entail important ramifications extending to all areas of military and political affairs. A major successful disarmament agreement would imply a willingness on the part of both sides to forego the use of force. The common recognition of the dangers inherent in the existence of weapons of mass destruction might significantly reduce the likelihood of local aggression.

The existence of a less extensive but major arms-control agreement would reduce the danger of local war by creating an added cost involved in launching aggression. Arms-control agreements will remain in effect only if both sides continue to find them valuable and desirable. In deciding whether to increase tensions or initiate local wars, both sides would have to weigh in the balance of costs and risks the possibility that the local aggression would cause the breakdown of the strategic arms control. For a number of reasons it might be true that an arms-control agreement could not, and would not, survive a local war. One of the reasons is psychological—simply that the atmosphere required for the continuation of arms control may have been spoiled. Both sides might accept arms control with the tacit assumption that it can go on only so long as there are no other major violations of international law. Insofar as any arms-control agreement was intended by both sides or one side to symbolize the end of crises, the agreement might simply cease to exist when a crisis came on. But there are other reasons why local war might mean the end of arms control.

One of these has already been mentioned. Arms control might well provide a cover for activities made illegal by the central war arms-control agreement. Insofar as the continuation of the agreement depended on both sides' being reassured that the other was in fact observing the agreement, local war might substantially upset the calculations as to the efficiency of the inspection system. As was suggested earlier it is likely to be much easier to hide illicit activity amidst the general confusion of preparation for war. In addition local war is likely to see the production on a large scale of weapons and weapon systems that are relatively easy to convert into strategic systems. For example, the production of tactical nuclear weapons to be used either in a local war or simply to be available in case the local war should become nuclear would be a case in point. Small tactical nuclear weapons can rapidly and readily be converted into large strategic weapons, and hence would bring into precarious balance any system of inspection to prevent the production of strategic nuclear weapons.

A closely related point is that many of the arms-control or ancillary arrangements might be violated or abandoned as a necessary concomitant of fighting a war. Agreements regarding the use, disposition, production, or testing of nuclear weapons would be hard to maintain while a nuclear war was in process or in its aftermath. Inspection of military posture and movements might be intolerable in time of war. Because of the dual purpose—tactical and strategic nature—of some weapon systems, both sides might have to violate a strategic arms-control agreement in order to fight a local war.

But even inspectors and inspection systems which do not interfere directly with the local-war effort might be politically intolerable in a situation of warfare. The presence of Chinese or even Russian inspectors on an American strategic-missile base, for example, would be a genuine political embarrassment during an attempted invasion of Taiwan. In time of threat of the use of force, democracies might find it politically embarrassing to allow observers from countries threatening them to continue to operate on their territory. In addition to the psychological and internal political difficulties, there might be a genuine fear that inspectors would serve as spies and couriers for purposes other than the ones for which they were in the other country. This is likely always to be the case. Inspection is always a genuine source of fear and difficulty, but this is likely to be particularly acute during a local war.

Finally, the occurrence of local war might lead both sides to reevaluate the desirability of stabilizing the strategic balance. The United States, for example, might accept the neutralization of the strategic balance with one or two thoughts in mind: both sides would refrain from lesser forms of violence; or it was capable with its allies of coping with local aggression with local force. Continuous successful use of local violence or threats of violence by the Soviet Union might lead the United States to decide that it simply cannot accept a world in which strategic forces were so stabilized and equalized that the world had been made safe for Communist aggression. The United States might be forced into a position where it decided to renounce the agreement and attempt to use threats of strategic force, however credible they are, and to rely on the danger of the explosion of local war to deter limited aggression.

During the period in which a strategic arms-control agreement was in effect, one or both sides might from time to time threaten to abrogate the agreement in the event of local aggression or threats of the use of force by the other power. An arms-control agreement is likely in this way to become a pawn of international power politics. Both sides might find this intolerable, feeling that if an arms-control agreement cannot be isolated from the general everyday threats of local war and aggression then it is not worth having. If the threat of breaking the agreement is to be constantly in the air, if either side oversteps what the other considers to be legitimate bounds of international action, then one or both sides might prefer to break the agreement rather than to remain in a situation in which both are constantly alert and sensitive to the danger of breakdown.

Strategic arms control then might not survive the initiation of local aggression or threats of the use of force. This might be because one or both sides, after balancing the costs and gains (discussed previously) of continuing the agreement, might simply decide to break the agreement deliberately. Or the agreement might break down without a clear-cut decision by one or both sides to break it. The agreement might simply slowly cease to be operative as a result of a series of threats of the use of force or of the actual outbreak of a local war. Thus, deliberately or inadvertently, strategic arms control might break down. Both sides might recognize this and so highly value the continued existence of the arms-control agreement that they would refrain from initiating local aggression and seek to restrain their allies.

The foregoing discussion assumed that strategic arms-control agreements were reversible. That is, an agreement once signed could be broken with a return to the *status quo ante*. Thus both sides would have to recognize that if they carried out an action which led to the breakdown of the arms-control agreement, they would return to the pre-arms-control state of a relatively unstabilized nuclear balance and a constantly perceived danger of strategic war. However this might not always be the case. It would be true most obviously for agreements which depended for the maintenance of the stability of the strategic balance on inspectors and inspection systems. A strategic balance, which both perceived would only remain stable (or as stable as the agreements it depended on) with the continued presence of inspectors, would be very susceptible to the kinds of pressures discussed and might well deter limited aggression.

On the other hand, there might be some sorts of arms-control agreements of which the major impact was irreversible. If both sides had discussed with each other the problems and meaning of well-protected, "second-strike" forces, and both had developed nonaccident-prone forces of this kind, the world might continue to appear safe for local wars even if the formal agreement were abrogated. Of course, such a system could be upset by a technological breakthrough, but probably so could the agreement with inspection.

It was suggested in Chapter 2 that unilateral action by both sides which created an extremely stable strategic balance would enhance the likelihood of local wars. An arms-control agreement by which both sides acknowledge their understanding of the existence of a stable balance and commit themselves to the adoption of well-protected, controlled forces would probably go even further in this direction. Even this sort of arms-control agreement will have some restraining effect on local war. Local war still might lead to the breakdown of the formal parts of the agreement and cause both sides to engage in a frantic production of missiles, a resumption of U-2-type activities, or a frantic research and development program. But the deterrence of local war by an arms-control agreement will vary depending on whether the agreement's stabilizing effect depends on its continued existence.

One of the major deterrents to local wars in a period of strategic arms control is the threat to break the arms-control agreement should a local war break out. This involves, in some sense, a paradox. Central-war arms-control agreements are designed precisely for those periods when the prospect of central war sharply increases. To some extent such agreements are in stand-by most of the time for use in the periods when the possibility of central war has gone up. However this is not necessarily inconsistent. As Schelling [258, p. 203] has suggested, arms-control agreements should be designed to take into account the fact that they may have to survive local wars and other crises. For example, neutral inspectors rather than Soviet or Chinese inspectors might be employed in the hope that neutral inspection might be possible during a local war while, as suggested earlier, inspection by teams from the current enemy are not likely to be acceptable. Nevertheless, despite the best efforts to have the arms-control agreement, as well as the stability of the strategic balance, survive a crisis or local-war period, both would inevitably be put in jeopardy by the starting of a local war. While an agreement, then, should be designed to try to avoid the possibility of its breakdown during a local-war period, the possibility will nevertheless persist and should be a restraint on countries desiring to maintain strategic arms control.

In addition to the fact that a desire to maintain a strategic arms-control arrangement may deter both sides from starting a local war, there is an additional factor which suggests that local wars may be less likely in a period of strategic arms control. Strategic arms control, in making clearer the inadequacies which to a large extent already exist in the alternative strategies for local defense, might improve the argument in favor of larger conventional forces. There is another reason why strategic arms control might lead to larger local-defense forces. A second argument which has been offered against the buildup of local forces is that they had to constitute a second priority claim on the American defense budget. It has been argued that the first claim must be on strategic forces large enough and effective enough to deter a Soviet attack. Thus, with an inevitably limited defense budget, local-war expenses have been held down because of the increasing cost of strategic war forces. Although some forms of arms control may increase expenditures rather than reduce them, successful central-war arms control, over the long run, would lead to a substantial decrease in expenditures for strategic forces. This is true primarily because even if the agreement provided no ceiling on the number of forces that either side could have, if both became confident that strategic forces had in fact been neutralized, if both were confident that the other side would not engage in a missile-production arms race, both sides would be likely to reduce their anticipated production of strategic forces. And, over the long run, expenditures for strategic-war preparations might significantly decline. If this money were still available for defense purposes, it could lead to increased expenditures for local-war forces. Moreover a strategic arms-control agreement which implied the neutralization of nuclear weapons would probably lead to increased expenditure on conventional matériel for local-war forces, which, it was suggested in Chapter 4, would probably increase their effectiveness.

There is the possibility, however, that strategic arms control would not lead to larger local-war forces. This largely depends on the attitude which the Administration and Congress take toward the signing of a strategic arms-control agreement. If the signing of such an agreement is taken as the end of the cold war, the end of potential threats of force and use of force by the Soviet Union and China, then it is likely to lead to greatly reduced defense budgets. Even if only the public and Congress take this view of arms control, there may be downward pressures on the defense budget. If strategic arms control in fact generates pressures which make local wars more likely and yet the United States does not counteract this by increased preparations for local war, countries which feel that they can no longer be protected either by American strategic forces or by American ground forces may cave in even without overt Communist aggression.

The effect on the American defense budget seems to be by far the most important determinant of whether strategic arms control makes local war more likely. The other major determinant is likely to be the nature of the agreement. An agreement which depends for stability on continued inspection and other overt cooperation is likely to be much more effective in deterring local aggression and threats of force than an agreement which stabilizes without the need for continuous inspection and other forms of overt cooperation.

Thus, if the United States does not take the necessary steps, the probability of local war is almost certain to rise. If the Administration remains alert to the fact that arms control on one level does not mean the end of the possibility of the use of force and threats of force on other levels, and if it takes the appropriate counteracting steps, then the danger of local aggression may decline—it need not rise.

## Fighting a Local War

Should local war break out in a period in which a strategic arms-control agreement is in effect, there are two distinct possible outcomes. One is that the arms-control agreement survives and the war is fought out under the umbrella of a strategic balance of continuing arms control. The other is that the agreement is abrogated by one or both sides or simply breaks down.

If the agreement breaks down, particularly if it is one which depended on a continuing inspection, then the breakdown is likely to lead to a period of great instability. In addition to whatever is taking place on the local battlefield, both sides will be vitally concerned with altering their strategic postures and strategic capabilities to accommodate themselves to the fact that the arms-control agreement, which they had relied upon in part for their protection, had been abrogated. In such a situation both sides may find it necessary to extricate themselves from their involvement in the local war in order to concentrate their attention on rebuilding their strategic forces. They may be unwilling to waste resources, men, and attention in fighting in the local area. In addition, with the sudden instability of the strategic balance, both sides may well feel that it is too risky to increase their stakes in a local war.

But, despite the psychological and political pressures to denounce an arms-control agreement in the event of local war, both sides may in fact be afraid of doing so for several reasons. First, both will realize that in the period of instability caused by the outbreak of local war the strategic arms control is even more important than it was previously. Both sides may so desperately want to avoid the danger of war by preemption that they are willing to tolerate the continuation of the arms control. Agreements may have to be modified to take into account the current overt hostility; they might also be modified in ways that improve control over strategic forces and reduce the danger of war by preemption. Both sides may find it impossible to break the arms-control agreement without seeming to signal to the other side that they are about to attack the other's homeland. That is, it might be difficult to break the agreement without greatly increasing the danger of a preemptive strike from the other side. In the period of tension caused by the outbreak of local war both sides might be very reluctant to carry out an action which would seem to be a signal that central war was about to begin.

Thus strategic arms control might survive and continue through the fighting of a local war. If it does so it is likely to affect the way in which the war is conducted. The effect of the arms arrangement will vary largely, depending on how fragile the agreement is and how much both sides are depending for their protection on the kinds of temporary international arrangements established by the agreement. If the agreement is a very fragile one that, if broken, would produce relative instability, then the conduct of the war is likely to resemble, in some ways, the conduct of a war with an unstable strategic balance.* In this case it will not be the strategic balance itself, but rather the arms-control agreement, which is so fragile that both sides act cautiously. In such a war, then, both of the major powers may well do everything they can to keep the war small, to isolate the military encounter from being a direct confrontation between East and West, to make the clash seem like a war with local issues rather than a war of the kind that clearly involves a military confrontation between the two major powers. Fighting the war this way may make it possible psychologically and politically to maintain arms agreements.

On the other hand, if the strategic balance has been stabilized by unilateral action and by arms-control agreements which are irreversible, then the effect of the strategic balance on the fighting would be similar to that of a stabilized strategic balance.† It would be a stable strategic balance further reinforced by certain discussions, mutual cooperation,

* See Chapter 1, pp. 11–13.
† See Chapter 1, pp. 13–15.

and understandings, which let both sides have more confidence in the fact that the balance was, in fact, stabilized. In such a situation both sides might be willing to fight a larger war, take greater risks, expand the war with some confidence that they would not touch off a preemptive strike by the other side.

It is important, then, to be clear on the need to explore the implications of any arms-control agreement for both its direct and indirect effects on local war and to note that even if one is trying to deal with some other problem—the stability of the strategic balance, the spread of nuclear weapons to other countries, the reduction of international tensions—one is also altering the local war balance in ways that may be decisive.

## LOCAL-WAR ARMS CONTROL

The relationship between arms control and local war may be much more direct than was suggested in the foregoing. Whether inadvertently or not, virtually any arms-control agreement will have direct as well as indirect effects on the local-war balance. Whether a particular agreement is aimed primarily at stabilizing the strategic balance, dealing with political-military problems, or directly affecting local war, it will have direct consequences for the deterrence and fighting of local war which need to be considered.

Although it is widely thought that central war is sufficiently costly to both major powers so there is a clear common interest in measures to make it less likely, particularly in measures to make inadvertent central war less likely, local war is less obviously something that neither side can "win." Thus both sides may not have an incentive to agree to arms-control agreements which reduce the likelihood of all local wars. There are, however, important possibilities of major-power local war that it might be in the joint interest to reduce through measures taken jointly. That is, although at certain points in time the Communist bloc may have positive incentives to initiate local aggression, there may be other times and other places when there is a joint interest in reducing the danger of local war. This is particularly likely to be true of those local wars which might start even though neither major power intends them to. If local war might be started by an "incident," measures to avoid incidents would be helpful. If particular members of the major-power blocs might initiate war that would drag the major powers in, measures to restrain allies might be jointly undertaken. If the mere existence of military forces in particular areas increases the likelihood of both sides' getting into military action they both deplored, measures to synchronize withdrawal might be helpful.

The major powers also have an interest in preventing wars among minor uncommitted nations. One goal of American policy certainly is to prevent war and bloodshed anywhere. But in the thermonuclear age both sides must be interested in preventing wars that may pull them in and lead ultimately to central war. (Scenarios for accidental central war often begin with a small-power clash.) Both major powers may also want to reduce the ability of third countries to bargain East against West. For several reasons, then, both the United States and the Soviet Union may have a strong interest in agreements that reduce the likelihood of local wars and wars among uncommitted nations.

Measures to prevent local and small-power wars might take a number of forms, both formal and informal. A joint arms embargo to a particular region might result from a policy announced by one side of not shipping arms if the other does not, or, alternately, from an international treaty. Arms embargoes may relate to particular countries (for example, Laos) or continents (for example, Africa). They may deal with all war matériel or just certain weapons. One of the functions, for example, of an agreement not to supply nuclear weapons to third countries would be to reduce the danger in local wars. Agreements by the major powers not to ally themselves with particular countries or factions may occasionally serve to quarantine an area, thus reducing the danger both of war and of war's expanding.

In addition at least some of the earlier discussion of the "open-skies" inspection arrangements and a discussion of surprise-attack inspection in 1961 can be interpreted as concerned with local-war surprise attacks. Also one can envisage an arrangement for the military neutralization, for example, of Quemoy and Matsu which would not imply that either side had given up their intention to use force in the Taiwan Straits area.

Arms-control agreements also might be aimed at agreeing on force levels for the two sides. An agreement that succeeded in establishing parity in ground forces might reduce the likelihood of overt military aggression, since offensive action generally requires a manpower advantage over the defensive. Such an agreement would not affect irregular warfare where this factor does not apply. Since guerrilla forces are more difficult (if not impossible to regulate) a force-level agreement might increase their power vis-à-vis the reduced Western conventional forces. Arms-control agreements which reduce the size of standing armies might reduce the magnitude of local wars should they come. However acceptance of this kind of agreement in contradistinction to agreement aimed explicitly at limiting local wars might imply that the forces would not be used. Just as strategic arms-control agreements would probably imply that strategic forces could not be used, so an agreement that stabilizes conventional forces at a particular force level might imply that such forces would not be used in a local war. Certainly it might be very difficult for a force-level agreement to survive even a local war between East and West.

Various proposals for disengagement in particular parts of the world, particularly in Europe, also seem to be designed primarily to reduce the dangers of local war's breaking out. However, all arms-control measures are not necessarily desirable, nor do they necessarily accomplish what they seek to. For example, although many who favor disengagement do so because they feel that it would reduce the likelihood of war in Europe, many disengagement plans might well increase the danger of war. While at certain times contact between troops produces friction which may lead to war, "no man's lands"—zones without troops—are also likely, in some cases, to produce war. If disengagement implied a reduced American commitment to defend continental European countries, it might lead to war. If disengagement meant withdrawal of Soviet troops from satellites which led to satellite revolts, it might make local war more likely. This suggests that all agreements which try to reduce the danger of local war may not succeed in doing so, and that an agreement which did reduce the danger of local war might have other implications which made it undesirable.

Some arms control aimed at preventing local wars without requiring political settlements might prove to be more easily carried out than arrangements dealing directly with the strategic balance. Cooperation in this area can more easily be informal and produces less difficult inspection and regulation problems. In addition the joint interest may be easier to embody in a concrete agreement.

## Limiting Local War

In local war certain military actions may not be taken specifically because of the anticipated response of the other side. Agreements, understandings, or restraints during local war might be negotiated either in peacetime or during the war. They might involve arrangements to be put in effect before or after the war breaks out. One can envision arms-control measures (designed to facilitate the limiting of war) which went into effect before the war—for example, an agreement not to produce any small tactical nuclear weapons. Other agreements might be designed to go into effect after war broke out—for example, agreements to maintain channels of communication in the event of a local war. Both sides might agree that during wartime they would allow their fissionable material stockpiles to be inspected, perhaps by neutrals, to make clear that they were not prepared to use such weapons in the war.

As was suggested in Chapter 1, there are two aspects to keeping a local war limited. The first is to maintain the stability of the strategic balance so that neither side feels compelled or tempted to initiate central war. The other is to arrive at the limits and restraints that stop the expansion of the war. Local war may put the stability of the strategic balance to a severe test. There may be an increased danger that both sides would decide that war had become so likely that it was necessary to preempt. Accidents of various kinds which might lead to the decision to launch central war are more likely during a local war. Thus agreements that reduce the incentive to preempt, the incentive to premeditated attack, and the danger of accidental war would all serve to help keep local wars limited, because of the contribution that they would make to the stability of the strategic balance.

Arms understandings can also contribute to keeping local wars limited by facilitating the process of restraining the activities of the participants. The process of limiting war may require some explicit or tacit bargaining, and arms understandings reached before the war would facilitate this process. Prewar arrangements may simply involve United States-Soviet discussions, formal or more likely very informal, of the nature of local war. Such communication of views would make it clear to each side that the other accepted the notion of the limited use of force in the nuclear-missile age. It could mean that if a local war did break out, neither would regard it as requiring a strategic nuclear response. Such discussion might also facilitate the explicit or implicit negotiations leading to recognized limits which might take place after the war broke out. Unilateral discussion of local war, such as has been going on in the United States, can also serve this goal by making American attitudes toward local war clear to the Soviet Union, and suggesting the way that America would pursue limits if war did break out.

In effect, during every local war, arms-control agreements are constantly being made, explicitly or implicitly; each side is deciding not to do certain things. There may be a cost involved in agreeing to measures which serve to facilitate keeping local wars limited. Just as agreements to stabilize the strategic balance may make local wars more likely, so agreements which serve to facilitate keeping local wars limited may make the outbreak of such wars more likely. If one of the things that prevents local wars is the fear of both sides that they will explode into central war, then agreements which make this less likely may result in making local war more likely. On the other hand, this could be a reasonable price for assurance that local war will not explode.

Arms-control agreements, both explicit and implicit and prewar and intrawar, might exploit this perceived common interest to produce a decreased likelihood that a local war would expand by establishing rules for the fighting of local wars. In order to do this, interrelation between military policy and arms-control negotiations and agreements must be appreciated. Too frequently the two policies have developed in isolation without an understanding of the way in which they affect each other. The problems and opportunities of the interaction between arms-control agreements and the establishment of rules for local war which have been discussed in this chapter can best be illuminated by considering a particular example. Since the most likely area for the use of arms control in establishing rules for local war is the question of the use of nuclear weapons in such wars, this question will now be considered.

## The Role of Nuclear Weapons

American policy on the use of nuclear weapons in local war should be closely related to its arms-control policy. As the previous chapter concluded, the United States should emphasize a conventional war strategy. If the United States does adopt such a strategy, arms-control negotiations and agreements should be employed to enhance the likelihood that a local war would remain conventional. On the other hand, if the United States decided that it wanted to use nuclear weapons in local wars, then steps should be taken in arms-control negotiations to indicate this fact, and to make it more likely that a nuclear war would not explode. Policy pressures operate both ways. Should the United States decide for other reasons that a proposal inhibiting the use of tactical nuclear weapons was desirable, it should alter its military policies. That is, if, for reasons connected with its desire to stabilize the strategic balance or to enhance long-range political objectives, the United States should accept an arms-control agreement which reduced the likelihood that a nuclear war could remain limited or which suggested that the use of nuclear weapons in local war would be inhibited by the fear of disrupting the arms-control agreement, then the United States should alter its strategy for local defense to take account of these facts. However, equally, if not more, important is the effect decisions on military policy should have on arms-control agreements and negotiations. If the United States settled on a nuclear local-war strategy it should use arms-control negotiations to facilitate this strategy and not to hinder it.

The relationship between arms control and rules for local war, and in particular, the use of nuclear weapons in local war, will be illustrated by discussing several proposed arms-control agreements. The nuclear-test ban dominated the arms-control scene for several years, but the close connection between the test ban and nuclear local war was not made clear in most discussions of the desirability or undesirability of a test ban. Many of those who opposed a test ban did so at least partly because of the desire to improve the tactical nuclear arsenal of the United States; most supporters of a ban ignored this issue even though it is of critical importance. If, as was argued in the preceding chapter, nuclear war is not easy to limit, and is not to the advantage of the West, then the United States would have an interest in a ban which might cut off developments such as "clean" bombs (pure fusion weapons) which might make nuclear weapons seem more conventional, and hence more likely to be used in a local war.

In addition to the direct effect of stopping the development of small-scale tactical weapons, a test ban would have other psychological effects which would inhibit the use of nuclear weapons. It would affect the expectations of both sides by making clear that both considered nuclear weapons to be somehow different. It would imply a joint recognition that such weapons are not "conventional" and would reinforce the expectation that they would not be used in a local war, increasing the stabilizing value of the nuclear-nonnuclear line. In addition, insofar as both sides wanted to keep a test ban in force, they would likely refrain from the use of nuclear weapons, because even if a test ban could survive any local war (which is by no means clear) it almost certainly could not survive nuclear war.

Finally, a test ban would probably make other agreements more likely. A number of possible arms-control agreements which have been proposed would have an even greater effect than the test ban on the use of nuclear weapons in local war.* The United States might, for example, simply make a unilateral declaration that it will not use nuclear weapons first, and suggest that the declaration will remain in force if the Soviets reciprocate. Alternatively the United States might seek a formal treaty which bars the use of nuclear weapons in local defense.†

The purpose of a formal treaty would be to seek to reinforce the present disposition of the major powers not to use nuclear weapons in local wars. There would seem to be a net advantage to the United States

* For a discussion of a program to neutralize nuclear weapons, see Read [242].
† For an extended evaluation of this proposal, see Halperin [104].

to transform this tacit understanding into a formal agreement. However, even the formal adoption of this proposal by the United States and the Soviet Union might not substantially reduce the likelihood that nuclear weapons would be used in a local war. Unlike an agreement which eliminates capability and provides an inspection system which indicates that the capability has been eliminated, the adoption of this proposal would have no short-run effect on the capability of the two sides to use nuclear weapons in a local war. If the agreement is to have immediate effect, then, it must affect their intentions and expectations.

The establishment of a formal agreement creates an additional cost if the rule is violated. Not only must each side calculate its costs and gains in using nuclear weapons, but the government also must estimate the costs in breaking an agreement in terms of establishing future agreements and in terms of its position in the eyes of its adversary, neutrals, and its allies. This may not be an overriding consideration, but, in a close decision, it may be marginally crucial at least for the West. In addition the proposal to break a treaty will probably force a more calculated decision. Even more than at present, strictly military aspects of the decision may be deemphasized and the role of political decision makers increased. In addition an agreement will reduce the likelihood of nuclear weapons' being used in a local war because the preemptive urge, which even in a local encounter is one of the strongest motives for the use of nuclear weapons, will be dampened. Since the side which uses nuclear weapons first is likely to gain an important advantage, one of the motives for use is the fear that the other side is about to use the weapons. If one becomes convinced that the nuclearization of the war is inevitable, then there is much to be gained on the battlefield by being the first to use nuclear weapons. Thus an agreement which reduced each side's expectation that nuclear weapons would be used by the other, an agreement by which each side signaled to the other that it did not intend to use nuclear weapons, might be important in quelling the preemptive urge to use nuclear weapons. Such an agreement might be valuable in discrediting the arguments of those who urge that nuclear weapons be used in order to anticipate their use by the other side.

Proposals for nuclear-free zones in Europe, Africa, or the Far East have been made from time to time. Such agreements would presumably bar the use of nuclear weapons within the zone of the agreement and would contribute to the expectation that the nuclear weapons would not be used anywhere in a local war. Another proposal which might enhance the possibility of keeping a local war conventional is to cut off the production of nuclear weapons. Action might be unilateral, with the United States simply announcing that it was stopping the production of nuclear weapons and would permit inspectors, either neutral or Soviet, to monitor compliance with the declaration. Or the United States might make its renunciation dependent on reciprocal renunciation by the Soviet Union. Alternatively the United States might seek a formal international agreement banning the production of fissionable material. Such agreement presumably would include some form of international inspection. These proposals should at least suggest the kind of arms-control agreements which might enhance the possibility of keeping a local war nonnuclear.

On the other hand, should the United States adopt a policy of using nuclear weapons in any local war, it should seek to enhance this policy in its arms-control arrangements. As Kissinger has pointed out, if the United States is relying on the use of nuclear weapons for local defense, it should refuse to engage in any arms-control negotiations which even tacitly imply that nuclear weapons are immoral or different [162, pp. 7-9]. More positively the United States might, in this case, seek agreements with the Soviet Union which would contribute to the stability of nuclear wars and reduce the political costs of using nuclear weapons.

These proposals have been sketched briefly not to suggest that the United States should necessarily seek to implement any or all of them, but only to indicate the general interaction between arms-control negotiations and agreements and military strategy, in particular, in relation to the role of tactical nuclear weapons.

An arms-control agreement dealing with this problem could take a number of forms as has been the case with the suspension of nuclear tests. Several arms-control arrangements banning the testing of nuclear weapons have been implemented and discussed, and each one of them, to a greater or lesser degree, would have the effects just discussed.

Initially the suspension of nuclear tests developed from unilateral statements by both sides that they were prepared to suspend testing as long as the other side did likewise. At the Geneva negotiations this was formalized to the extent that both sides recognized each other's unilateral declaration and agreed that they would keep them both in force. Later the United States indicated that it no longer considered its pledge in force, but that it would nevertheless from day to day suspend the testing of nuclear weapons and would announce in advance any decision to resume testing. The negotiations at Geneva sought to produce a formal international treaty obligating the signers not to test nuclear weapons. Also at Geneva the two sides considered a moratorium for underground tests which would be a less formal international agreement under which both sides would pledge not to test nuclear weapons.

This spectrum suggests that arms-control agreements seeking to establish any particular rule for the fighting of a local war may take a number of forms.

It is important to keep clearly in mind the process involved in using arms control in helping to limit and structure local wars.* The first question to be asked is what rules are we interested in establishing (for example, nuclear weapons should not be used in local wars). We should then try to make the rule as concrete and as operational as possible (for example, neither side shall introduce nuclear weapons in the defense of local areas). It is only then that we can come to the problem of how do we get the rule, and of particular relevance here, how can we use arms-control negotiations and agreements to help to establish the rule.

In addition to preventing the use of nuclear weapons, there may well be other rules for the fighting of local wars that the United States could seek to establish by the use of arms-control negotiations and agreements. In each case, the United States should first decide what the rule is that it wishes to establish—neither Russian nor American soldiers will be used on local battlefields; diplomatic relations and direct contact will be maintained during a local war; and so on. Having determined the desirable rules for local war, the United States should formulate them as clearly as possible. Then various possible unilateral or formal arms-control approaches should be explored to see which might contribute most to establishing the rule. Any arms-control proposal which seems desirable from this point of view would then have to be evaluated for its other military and political implications before it would be wise to pursue it as American policy.

* For an elaboration of this approach to arms control, see Fisher [80, pp. 56–67].

# 6

# The Limitation of Central War

WHILE VIRTUALLY ALL of the literature on limited war has focused on the possibilities and problems of restraining a local war between East and West, central as well as local war may be limited.

The most likely limitation in a central war involves targets attacked. The limit might be quantitative with each side attacking some but not all of a particular type of target—for example, attacking some strategic forces but deliberately not trying to destroy all of them. But here qualitative limitation is also a possibility; one side or both might deliberately avoid destruction of a particular class of targets. Both sides might decide to avoid strategic targets and engage purely in counter-population attacks, either quantitatively restrained or not. One or both sides might also engage in attacks only on strategic forces, again either quantitatively limited or unrestrained. However, because in some cases strategic forces are in close proximity to large population centers, it may not be possible to avoid population damage unless a deliberate effort is made to do so. In discussion of bombing cities, four approaches each side might take may be distinguished:

1. A decision to strike deliberately at major population centers.

2. A decision to strike deliberately only at strategic forces, ignoring the question of whether this would involve major civilian casualties, and not altering the methods of destruction (that is, air-burst rather than ground-burst) in order to reduce the civilian casualties.

3. A decision to take into consideration the desire to avoid civilian casualties as one factor to be weighed in determining the targets to attack.

4. A decision not to attack any targets which cannot be bombed without causing a large number of civilian casualties and to air-burst rather than ground-burst nuclear weapons targeted on sites near population centers to reduce the civilian casualties.

## ALTERNATIVE STRATEGIES

By combining various qualitative and quantitative restraints one can conceive a number of possibilities for limiting central war. Much discussion of central war has assumed that there would be no restraint, that both sides would fire all their weapons as quickly as possible against all targets in the opposing country. However, when attention is focused on limitation, three distinct kinds of limited war have been identified and discussed.

1. *Limited Retaliation.* This strategy involves a quantitative and qualitative restraint as to targets and a quantitative restraint as to weapons. It is generally thought of as a policy calling for the attacking only of cities or other nonmilitary targets [139]. One can also conceive a limited retaliation exchange in which both sides attack single strategic sites rather than cities. It is possible to imagine qualitative restraint in which both sides refrained from attacking both large population centers and missile sites and concentrated on targets such as oil fields, gaseous diffusion plants, staging bases, or missile test ranges which were not prime strategic targets but also did not involve large population destruction.* This strategy involves severe quantitative restraint. Both sides fire very few missiles, perhaps one at a time, increasing to larger numbers if one side does not back down after the initial exchanges.

2. *Countercity.* Under this category is envisioned a central war which may involve little or no quantitative restraint on the use of strategic forces, but which involves qualitative restraint involving attacks only on cities and not on strategic forces. Frequently, this is advocated as a prewar-threat position, not necessarily indicating how a war actually should be fought. The primary motivation for limiting one's threats to countercity threats and perhaps altering one's forces so that they appear to be capable only of countercity operations is that this dampens the danger of preemption. If each side can effectively attack only by attacking cities, neither has any incentive to go first.†

* The purpose here would be to demonstrate determination and resolve without touching off a preemptive strike by the other side.
† This strategy is frequently identified as "stabilized deterrence." For the arguments that this dampens the danger of preemption, see Schelling [261, pp. 233–

3. *No Cities.* In contradistinction to the previous category, central war here involves attacks only on strategic targets. In this situation each side attacks the other's strategic forces but does not deliberately seek to destroy civilian populations. The restraint is qualitative in the sense of avoiding cities and may be quantitative in that one does not fire all of one's missiles but holds some in reserve to threaten city destruction.

This is the strategy which Secretary of Defense Robert McNamara announced in June of 1962 that the United States has adopted. In a speech on NATO strategy at the University of Michigan commencement, Secretary McNamara declared:

> The United States has come to the conclusion that, to the extent feasible, basic military strategy in a possible general nuclear war should be approached in much the same way that more conventional military operations have been regarded in the past. That is to say, principle military objectives, in the event of a nuclear war stemming from a major attack on the alliance, should be the destruction of the enemy's military forces, not of his civilian population.
> The very strength and nature of the alliance forces make it possible for us to retain even in the face of a massive surprise attack, sufficient reserve striking power to destroy an enemy society if driven to it. In other words, we are giving a possible opponent the strongest imaginable incentive to refrain from striking our own cities [192, p. 67].

The remainder of this chapter will focus on this variant of controlled central war which is currently American policy.*

## MOTIVES FOR LIMITATION

In attempting to describe each side's motivation for avoiding city destruction and observing quantitative restraint on the use of its strategic forces, two problems need to be considered: the effect on prewar objectives of the attempt to convey to the other side the adoption of such a strategy and the motivations for restraint once the war begins.

In the prewar situation, both sides have two classes of objectives. They want to deter central war and they desire to use strategic forces

---

237]. For many, this strategy is attractive because it seems to clear the way for significant reductions in strategic forces and the possibility of negotiated arms-control agreements. For this approach, see Frisch (editor) [83].

* For a discussion of the no-cities strategy, see Snyder [280, pp. 73–74] and Kahn [136, pp. 174–175].

to affect local wars. The latter problem was discussed previously, and only the former will be analyzed here.

In considering the problem of deterring a central war, it is important to distinguish wars in terms of their origin. The distinction of most relevance to deterrence is the choice the decision maker thinks he has at the time that he decides to strike. Is he choosing between central war or no central war, or is he choosing between striking first or striking second? In the case in which the decision maker chooses central war, the relevant question is why he decided to do so.

Two questions are relevant to the problem of the deterrence of preemptive central war. First, how would a controlled counterforce strategy affect the fear of a preemptive strike, and second, how would it affect the chances of a strike if an attack is expected? Trying to convince the Soviets that the United States will not strike first may be trying to persuade them of something that they are already certain about. On the other hand, their Marxist-Leninist image of the world may lead them to discount the factors which do seem to rule out the possibility of an American first strike. Given the circumstances in which both sides are conscious of the possibilities of central war, the Soviets may have residual fear that the United States will strike first. American officials seem to believe that the Soviets might strike first in some circumstances if they had a sufficient capability.

The side fearing a first strike might be less likely to feel a need to preempt if the strike it expected were a limited counterforce one. The government, if it feels its forces can survive, might see such a strike as making possible a victory without doing very major damage to its homeland. On the other hand, if a countercity attack were expected, there would be pressure to preempt to prevent the massive damage to population and industrial capacity which could be inflicted in a coordinated countercity first strike.

However a first strike may be considered more likely if its purpose was to destroy strategic forces. A first-strike, countercity attack, which left the opponent's missile force intact, might appear to put the attacker in such a poor position that the strategy would not be implemented. It is thus not clear whether a countercity or counterforce strategy is more likely to deter a preemptive attack by the United States or the Soviet Union.

In fact, it is not the particular strategy of each side but rather the vulnerability of strategic forces which is the major determinant of the danger of preemption. It is difficult to believe that the side which struck first would refrain from attacking the strategic forces of the other side which could be easily destroyed. Even if the United States had adopted a stabilized-deterrence, countercity strategy, it would not refrain from attacking vulnerable Soviet strategic forces should it be driven to beginning a central war. American decision makers also would not believe that the Soviets would avoid striking American vulnerable strategic forces should the Soviets begin a central war. Thus, in a situation in which both sides are vulnerable, both would recognize that their strategic forces might be destroyed and there might be an acute danger of preemption.

However, once one side moves, as the United States seems to have, into a position in which a large part of its force could not be taken out in a surprise attack, preemption does not seem to be a very serious danger. At the present time the Soviets have no incentive to preempt since even a well-executed, first-strike attack could not prevent their almost complete disarming—assuming theirs was a counterforce attack, nor virtual destruction of the Soviet Union—assuming they attacked Western cities. As long as there is any hope that the West is not about to strike, the Soviets are more likely to seize the option of reducing a local threat which is creating the danger of preemption, rather than themselves preempting. The United States, because of its relatively superior position, has little reason to preempt and much reason to try to discover ways to use its relative superiority to force the Soviets to withdraw their pressure in the local area.

Once both sides have invulnerable strategic forces the danger of preemption is low regardless of the strategies involved.

In terms of deterring a deliberate attack, the question is what will be the effect of indicating that the response to a first strike will be quantitatively restrained and qualitatively limited to strategic forces (if cities have not been attacked).

Given a situation in which the Soviets do not expect an attack from the United States and do not feel that they have the capability to destroy most of the American strategic force, they would have to have a very strong dislike of the nonwar situation to contemplate an attack. The Soviet leadership has acted cautiously and has been unwilling to jeopardize the continued existence of its rule in the Soviet Union; it has also acted decisively when necessary to save the Communist regime. It would probably require certainty of destroying the American strategic force for it to decide to initiate central war, unless continued Bolshevik rule in the Soviet Union were seen to be at stake. In such circumstances the Soviets might be willing to risk a central war if they felt that the war might save their regime—and no other course were available—by dampening the current danger and eliminating their major opponent.

Such a situation is not likely—it is in fact very difficult to imagine such circumstances coming about—but this situation seems to be the only one in which the Soviets would contemplate a deliberate first strike. In these circumstances the Soviets may be more deterred by a fear of losing the war than by the fear of the destruction of Soviet cities. The Soviets may feel that they have no choice but to accept very large-scale civilian destruction if the failure to act may jeopardize Bolshevik rule. They are more likely to be deterred by the belief that their action may lead to their defeat by the United States.

It is an open question as to whether a counterforce, a countercity, or a mixed American attack would seem to the Soviets to most jeopardize their control of Russia. However an American emphasis on winning a strategic war is more likely to deter a deliberate central war than the threat of city destruction per se.

## Intrawar Motives

The previous section assumed that the likelihood of central war may be influenced by the way in which we develop our strategic forces. Many people believe, however, that central war could only occur as a result of an accident or miscalculation; since no country would deliberately launch a nuclear war, it is useless to try to prevent a war by altering the prospective payoffs of the leaders of the major powers. From that perspective the discussion of how an emphasis on controlled counterforce affects the likelihood of war misses the point that such activity does not influence the probability of central war.

If the major powers were to adopt this perspective their interest in controlling central war should increase. For, in focusing on intrawar considerations, the American and Soviet interest in limitation is more obvious. Once deterrence fails neither side has any interest per se in destroying the other's homeland. Thus a major motivation for each side to exercise restraint during a central war is the desire to induce reciprocation by the opponent. If the Soviet leaders are not concerned with limiting damage to American cities, they may nevertheless want to limit damage to their own cities and their own industry and population. Both sides will also be concerned with maintaining control over their own territory, maintaining the regular functioning of government, and exercising control over their strategic forces to prevent their unauthorized use. Here again the desire for restraint by the opponent may lead to self-restraint.

Soviet and American leaders may also have a direct interest in insuring the survival of their opponent's civilian government and its control over strategic forces. Unless both sides are determined to fight out the war until all strategic forces have been employed, they will be as interested in having the enemy maintain control over his strategic forces as they are in maintaining control over theirs. The possibility of achieving a stalemate or a victory, or even of surrendering before the war runs its course, will depend on being able to negotiate a war-termination agreement with the other side and on the maintenance of military and civilian control of strategic forces, and communication between the ruling centers of the two powers.

In addition both sides may have a positive incentive not to strike at each other's cities. If central war comes there should be concern with utilizing strategic forces for the important task of destroying enemy strategic forces or for threatening punitive damage in the event of destruction of one's own cities. One side may at some point want to destroy some cities as a means of demonstrating resolve or seriousness or in retaliation for either accidental or deliberate destruction of one of its own cities. But it will never pay in terms of prevailing in a strategic war or reducing damage to one's own side to "waste" missiles in an attempt to destroy the opponent's industrial capacity or to kill his civilian population.

Whether internal and foreign political pressures play an inconsequential or dominant role in providing incentives for qualitative and quantitative limitation depends on the length and character of the central war. Both the American and Soviet populace and countries which are involved in the war or fear that they may be drawn in are likely to urge a termination of hostilities and an avoidance of city destruction. If the war is over quickly such pressures are not likely to have time to influence decision makers. At the other extreme, in a very slow limited-retaliation situation these pressures may be crucial. A Soviet limited-retaliation, counterpopulation attack may well be aimed at bringing these pressures to bear on the American and allied governments.

## INTERACTION

If a central war breaks out each side will have a strong incentive to limit its own actions and to seek reciprocal limitation from its opponent. Whether such limitation proves to be possible in the event will depend on decisions made and attitudes formed prior to the outbreak of the central war as well as the way in which the war develops.

A major factor in determining whether limitations are in fact observed by both sides will be the government's expectations about the possibility that a central war might be limited. As just suggested a major motivation for limitation will be to try to induce reciprocal limitation by the other side. Such a hope depends on the belief of each side that the other is at least considering limitation and might respond to one's own efforts to limit a central war. The feeling that reciprocal restraint is possible would be reinforced not only by a general feeling that the other side is alert to the possibility of restraint, but by the feeling that the two sides have a common notion of what kinds of restraints are possible during a central war.

Even if, as seems likely, the Soviets refuse to recognize explicitly the possibility of limitation in the event of central (or indeed local) war, it might still be possible for American leaders to develop a feeling that the Soviets did in fact understand the possibilities for limitation. Whether American leaders had such a feeling and whether in fact it accurately reflected Soviet beliefs would be an important factor in determining whether or not limitation was possible during the course of a war.

If the United States and the Soviet Union did not feel that the negotiated termination of the war would be possible, they would have less interest in maintaining channels of communication between the two sides and in preserving the means for internal communication. In addition one's image of the opponent's command and control structure may be important in determining whether one goes after his command capabilities. If one side feels that its opponent is able and willing to fight a restrained war, it might not try to interfere with its opponent's control over strategic forces.

In addition, of major importance will be the existing hardware on the two sides. The proper hardware will facilitate the limitation of central war, and the failure to provide the equipment may make limitation impossible. Of major importance is the development by each side of facilities enabling it to exercise tight command and control over its strategic forces and give them complicated orders. At least within the next several years one can preplan most of one's second strike regardless of what the enemy does in his first strike. Thus we may need to have the ability to give flexible orders to only a small part of the strategic force. A go/no-go setup might be sufficient for the rest. Unless the proper steps are taken the United States and the Soviet Union may be forced into an unrestrained central war because that is the only way they can use their strategic forces.

In addition to command and control facilities, strategic forces themselves must be equipped to carry out limited strikes. Good reconnaissance capabilities which indicate what targets in the enemy territory have been destroyed, and an ability to learn quickly what targets in the homeland have been attacked may facilitate mutual restraint. In addition, unless each side is sure of its ability to have at least a major part of its strategic force survive one or repeated strategic strikes, it may be forced to fire everything or see it destroyed by a continuing wave of strategic attacks.

The positioning of each side's strategic forces will be a major determinant of the likelihood of avoiding city damage. If either side has built its strategic forces very close to cities, it might be impossible for the other to adopt an attack posture which avoids large-scale city destruction.* Both sides might enhance the possibility of fighting a controlled counterforce war by building their strategic complexes far away from large population centers and constructing fallout shelters so that if both sides adopt the posture of simply not going after cities they may avoid causing large-scale civilian damage.

Finally, existing war plans will determine the kind of restraint that can be observed if a war breaks out. Although one can always decide not to fire some weapons, the implementation of a relatively complicated controlled strike would require the prior development of a plan. Once central war breaks out there will not be time to devise a new targeting and control system. This factor alone makes prewar attention to the need for restraint necessary if both sides are to fight in a controlled manner.

In addition to each side's image of the possibility of quantitative and qualitative restraint in central war and the hardware decisions that are taken in peacetime, the third major determinant of the likelihood of limiting a central war will be the process by which the war breaks out. Perhaps the dominant factor here will be the nature of the initial attack. If central war develops during a local war, it may be the result of slow expansion so that neither side is quite sure when the boundary has been crossed into central war. Hence each side may continue to react on an ad hoc basis to particular expansion by the opponent including expansions that involve strategic attack on its own homeland. In this case the prospects for limitation may be great. Each side, if it views the danger of preemption as being low, may see the strategic attacks as being aimed at influencing the outcome on the local battlefield and may respond accordingly without the initial fear that this was in fact the beginning of a major central war. Such exchange might continue to expand into a very large-scale war, but the decision to expand would be made serially, and a conscious decision would have to be made to launch an attack

* A side seeking to signal to the other its complete lack of interest in limiting central war might station its strategic forces within its largest cities.

with all or most of one's forces. In this situation both sides may feel that they can influence the strategic exchange not only be retaliation in kind but also by actions on the local battlefield including the possibility of surrender. The reason for the strategic attacks will be clear, the existence of limited war-termination conditions may be recognized, and hence the prospects for restraint enhanced.

On the other hand, should a central war break out when no local war is in progress, the prospects for limitation will be reduced. In such a situation the nature of the first strike might be crucial. If it were large and qualitatively unlimited, the prospects for a restrained blow from the other side would be low. On the other hand, if the strategic first blow were clearly limited, if it avoided the destruction of cities and seemed to be aimed at particular strategic targets, and if it should be accompanied by a statement of limited objectives, the prospects for limitation might be significant. If the proper prewar measures have not been taken, the defender may not be in a position to distinguish between a controlled counterforce attack and an all-out attack which included the targeting of major population centers. In part, of course, this will depend on the motives and calculations of the side launching the strategic first strike, but perhaps even more on the interpretation of it that the other side makes.

The process of limitation would be enhanced by direct communication between the two sides; however, such communication probably will not be carried on during the early hours of a strategic war. How quickly communication is established, on what basis, and what damage has been done, all will affect the degree to which the war can be kept controlled. In particular the possibility of agreeing on a comprehensive arms-control arrangement may enable both sides to end the war with the feeling that the intolerable conditions which led to the war would not persist. It would be impossible to develop such plans during a crisis or central war. The development within the American government of acceptable comprehensive arms-control systems and discussion of them with the Soviets would facilitate intrawar negotiations designed to bring the strategic exchange to a halt before cities had been targeted and would substantially reduce the danger of central war recurring.

## AMERICAN POLICY

There are a number of implications for American policy of emphasizing controlled counterforce action in the event of central war.

While of particular relevance to a no-cities posture, many of the proposals to be discussed would be of value even if the United States decided not to emphasize the possibility of restraint.

## Capability

In addition to being as invulnerable as possible, strategic forces should be under tight control. Provision should be made for the survival of the top civilian echelon in the government as well as of the communication from them to those who actually have physical control over the strategic forces. The possibility of unauthorized firing should be reduced as far as possible, and those who control the force should be given every confidence in the belief that their superiors will survive and will be passing them complex orders about the use of some or all of the strategic force. The strategic command should be prepared for orders to use only part of the force and to attack specific strategic targets. In addition the force should have a reconnaissance capability to enable the United States to assess the extent of Soviet damage. The reconnaissance capability may be carried out in part by satellite photographic systems, but there may also be a need for manned aircraft which could travel at a slow enough pace over the Soviet Union to do reconnaissance work. One of the functions of the planes might be to spot particular targets and destroy them. There is also a need for extremely accurate systems that can arrive at pretargeted locations and hunt out targets whose coordinates are not precisely known and destroy them.

Perhaps the most important criterion of a strategic force, whether or not one is interested in restraint, is the ability to survive through a crisis and remain invulnerable. We need a strategic force which the major civilian leaders are confident cannot be destroyed by the Soviets in a first strike or which does not lose its potency if made to hold over an extended period. The need for such qualifications rules out strategic systems which depend for their invulnerability on procedures which cannot be maintained over a long period of time.* We want strategic forces which do not depend for their survivability or their effectiveness on being in a top-alert status after which they become increasingly vulnerable. In addition the alert status should not appear provocative to the opposing side. Thus a major criterion for strategic forces is that they should be able to insure their invulnerability without doing things which increase their ability to attack the Soviet Union.

* This may be true, for example, of air-borne alert postures, depending on the nature of the planes, the amount of time they can stay in the air, the time they need between flights, and the procedures adopted.

The "optimum" size of an American strategic force has not been discussed. Whether the force needs to be very large or moderately small depends on a number of things, including our image of the degree to which the Soviet force is responsive to decisions we make about the size of American strategic forces. However the adoption of a no-cities strategy does not necessarily require the United States to go on building missiles at a continually accelerating rate. If the Soviets develop relatively invulnerable, hard, dispersed, or mobile missile systems, it simply will not pay for the United States to develop forces which might increase by a very small percentage the possibility of destroying a given percentage of the total Soviet missile force. The size of the American missile force is and must be, whatever strategy the United States has adopted, related to the size and quality of the Soviet force. The United States, by its adoption of a controlled counterforce strategy, has not inherently committed itself to maintaining a force which is as superior to the Soviet force as our current forces are. In fact, the cost of doing so would be prohibitive if the Soviets developed well-protected, sophisticated strategic forces. As long as they do not do so, the currently programmed American forces are sufficient to maintain American strategic superiority. If the Soviets decide to develop sophisticated, well-protected systems, they can make meaningful superiority impossible and enable a leveling off of the quantitative strategic-arms race even if both sides adopt a no-cities posture. The size of the American force cannot in any case be determined by something as simple as being able to guarantee that a given number of missiles survive, assuring the Soviets a given number of civilian casualties. We are not likely to want to carry out such a countercity attack, and as was suggested, this may not be the optimum deterring threat.

A fallout-shelter construction program would also facilitate restraint by making it easier for the Soviets to avoid civilian destruction in attacking strategic targets. Urban shelters thus complement the moving of strategic forces away from the large population centers in increasing the possibility of a qualitatively restrained central war.

## Communication of Intentions

As was suggested previously, limiting a central war may depend on both sides' believing that limitation is possible and that the other is likely to reciprocate restraint. The United States should continue to emphasize that the changes it is making in its strategic posture are relevant to the limitation of central war: for example, its increased control over its strategic forces, the location of these forces away from population centers, and its program for the construction of fallout shelters. The United States might also suggest that the Soviets take similar action and itself acknowledge actions by the Soviets which would contribute to the likelihood of limitation of central war even if the Soviets did not choose to publicly put this interpretation on their actions. We should act as if we believe that limitation is at least possible if central war breaks out.* The United States might spell out even more explicitly its commitment to particular kinds of limitations by stating more clearly than was done in the McNamara speech [192] that we would not target cities unless the Soviets did so, and we might privately suggest to the Soviets that they separate these two types of targets so that city destruction would not become necessary. The United States should stress the nonprovocative nature of its strategic forces, the fact that it is confident of their ability to ride out a Soviet attack, confident of the fact that it need not do anything which will appear provocative to the Soviets in a crisis.

Such a communication policy should go a long way toward damping the danger of a preemptive war in the event of a crisis or a local war. It should enable to the United States to act boldly in such situations without fearing the outbreak of central war, and, in particular, this communication policy would make possible the implementation of a limited-retaliation strategy should the Administration feel it necessary.†

## Action Policy

Given the capability and communication policy just outlined, what in fact should the United States plan to do in the event of central war or in the event that the American government decides to use its strategic forces to deal with local wars and crises?

Regardless of how central war breaks out and who initiates it, the United States should plan to fight in a way that permits the Soviets to limit their attack in response to our own restraint on the use of strategic forces. At least in the early stages of a central war, American strategic strikes probably should be extremely limited quantitatively and confined

* This kind of unilateral communications policy might take a form very similar to the developing American policy on local war; we talk about the possibility of limiting local war and act as if local war could be limited. Even though the Soviets continue to deny this, one suspects that both we and the Soviets now share a powerful belief in the possibility of limiting local war, a belief which might be spread to central war by similar actions on the part of the West.
† This is not meant to imply that limited retaliation is an optimum strategy for the West or one that is likely to redound to its benefit if the West decides to implement it.

to targets which do not involve large population damage. In addition, in some situations the United States might even want its initial attack, particularly if it were the first attack, to avoid any strategic targets at all, to be a punitive countermilitary or countereconomic strike rather than one that might trigger a jittery Soviet strategic force. The United States should in any case withhold a large part of the American strategic force in an attempt to bargain with the Soviets for the conclusion of the war as soon as possible without damage to America's vital interests. Except in certain very extreme situations, the United States ought to avoid any first use of strategic forces.

It is the current American quantitative superiority and the relative vulnerability of Soviet strategic forces that would enable the United States in a central war both to attack Soviet strategic forces and to hold a reserve to threaten Soviet city destruction. Given this balance it needs to be asked whether the Soviets would have any reason to agree to the adoption of a counterforce strategy by both sides. While in fact the Soviets are unlikely to publicly accept the no-cities strategy as long as their strategic forces are highly vulnerable to a Western attack, they would have a strong interest in observing limitations should war occur.

Given the current imbalance of strategic forces and even assuming that the United States struck first in a well-coordinated attack and the Soviets responded with a no-cities second strike, the collateral damage to the United States and its NATO allies would be sufficiently great that the Soviets could be confident of deterring an American attack "out of the blue." What the Soviets must now fear is that the West might, if pushed either in Berlin or in Central Europe as a whole, launch a strategic nuclear attack if the only alternative seemed to be defeat or a massive use of tactical nuclear weapons which would destroy Western Europe. This should give the Soviets an additional incentive to avoid massive pressure on the West. On the other hand, if the Soviets do not launch a major military threat to the West, they have sufficient force to deter an American first strike and absolutely no reason to contemplate an attack on the United States.

Should war nevertheless come by accident or miscalculation, the Soviets would share with the United States an interest in avoiding the destruction of cities and bringing the war to an end as quickly as possible. The extension of the war to city targets would involve much greater destruction in the Soviet Union than in the United States and the rest of the West, while the confinement of the war to military targets would probably result in greater civil damage in Western Europe and the United States combined than in the Soviet Union. Thus, even if a war came with the present strategic imbalance, the Soviets would have a massive incentive to fight a no-cities war although they may not acknowledge this in advance.

Should the Soviets, as a result of a threat of an American first strike which they claim to have read into the McNamara speech [192] or simply because they develop a better understanding of strategy, decide to develop better-protected and larger strategic forces, the controlled no-cities strategy would continue to be in the interests of both sides. In the case of relative qualitative and quantitative parity, neither the United States nor the Soviet Union, whether it went first or second, could hope to destroy the opponent's strategic forces. However both sides may continue to engage in attacks on the opponent's vulnerable forces or they might implement some variant of the limited-retaliation strategy discussed previously. Both sides will continue to have vulnerable targets such as airfields and radar sites which can be profitably attacked in a nuclear war. However, if both sides have strategic forces so hardened and dispersed that one only "wastes" missiles in attacking them, both sides may simply withhold very large parts of their strategic forces. If nuclear war occurs in a situation in which both sides have well-protected forces, a central war may be much slower than is now envisioned. It may involve attacks on strategic forces which are vulnerable or whose vulnerability is discovered or develops during the course of the war, or it may involve limited strategic strikes on tactical military targets, on airfields, or on economic targets such as oilfields which are not close to major population centers.

It should be recognized that it is in the interest of the United States to avoid attacking Soviet cities even if the Soviets strike first. While it is undoubtedly true that a counterforce attack would be more effective in a first-strike situation, it is nevertheless true that there will be a considerable number of counterforce targets in a second strike, including airfields from which planes have not yet taken off and staging bases at which planes might stop on the way to an attack or to which they might return after an attack to be reloaded and sent back. In addition, some missiles might not have fired on schedule and might still be targets. According to Hanson Baldwin the Soviets have the capability of firing two missiles from each launcher.* If this is so then missile launchers will be important targets even after the first missile has been fired. There are also a number of defensive targets which might be attacked, including antimissile sites or the radar for antiaircraft sites, fighter-interceptor airfields, communications (if it is decided to attack these), and perhaps tactical military targets if a local war is in progress. There will, then, be a number of urgent targets remaining after a Soviet first strike. De-

* New York Times, July 26, 1961, p. 1.

struction of these by the United States would reduce the Soviet capability to threaten civil damage on the United States while retaining the possibility of an ending of the war before large population centers are attacked.

It is impossible to lay out any precise rules for action policy in central war and difficult for the United States to plan in advance what it would do in particular situations in which it is faced with the need to initiate a strategic exchange or faced with a strategic attack by its opponent. The situation is likely to involve unanticipated attacks and problems, pressures, and objectives. The United States should maintain as much flexibility as possible, enough control over its strategic forces so that the top civilian leaders can decide what is the most appropriate policy. The United States should begin to think more carefully about ways in which central war might break out and thereby discover different ways in which it might want to implement a no-cities strategy. But, in any case, it is most certainly not going to discover the way in which the events would occur should a central war take place. The Administration should be prepared for the unexpected and have the capability to react to it in a way that seems most likely to contribute to limiting the war and enhancing other American objectives.

However, despite the efforts of the United States to develop a capacity to limit central war, in the event that it occurs, a central war may turn out to be the unlimited holocaust that many observers have asserted it must be. There can be no certainty that a central war can be limited. In fact, one must assume that it is likely that cities will be attacked before a central war comes to an end, and American efforts must be directed largely at the deterrence of any central war. Nevertheless prudence demands that every effort be made to limit a central war should it occur. Such efforts may fail but they are worth making.

## ARMS CONTROL

In most discussions of the problem, it is assumed that an arms-control policy is compatible only with what has come to be called stabilized deterrence. Arms control, it is argued, is only possible if the United States develops a small strategic force designed simply to deter a Soviet strike by threatening countercity retaliation. Regardless of whether an arms-control policy could be based on such a strategy, it should be clear that arms control is in no sense incompatible with a controlled no-cities strategy. This strategy might rule out, assuming it ever was a real possibility, a formal agreement on the size of strategic forces, but it would not rule out tacit bargaining between the two sides over the level or qualities of their forces. In fact, insofar as strategic forces are aimed at each other rather than at cities, they may be more responsive to the quality of the enemy's strategic force. If we concentrate on the fact that missiles comprise a war-fighting capability designed to destroy opposing strategic forces and to survive attacks from them, we are more likely to be aware of the relationship between the size of the two forces and responsive to possible limitations by the other side. Each side, however, may also be more responsive to pressures to out-produce the other side.

A decision by the United States to avoid city destruction and to seek to get the Soviets to reciprocate raises the possibility of an arms-control agreement, whether formal or informal, designed to insure the avoidance of city attacks in the event of central war. It is conceivable, although highly improbable, that the two sides could negotiate a formal agreement in which both sides commit themselves not to attack cities.* Although there would of course be no way of "enforcing" such an agreement in the event of central war, it would at least focus both sides' attention on the possibility of avoiding city destruction, and would make each side aware that the other would be conscious of its decisions in terms of avoiding cities or attacking them. Hence the agreement would significantly enhance the likelihood that both sides would strive to avoid city destruction in the event of central war.

Attempting to negotiate a formal agreement, however, might be counterproductive. Should the United States propose such an agreement, and the Russians reject the proposal, for whatever reason, it might be more difficult in the event of war for both sides to observe such a policy. In other words, the Soviets having formally rejected American overtures for an agreement to avoid cities, both sides may feel that this limitation is not likely to be observed in the event of central war. On the other hand, a tacit agreement may be established by informal discussion within the United States which is understood and tacitly accepted by the Soviets. In fact, the best way to establish an informal rule against destruction of cities may be simply for the United States to continue to indicate that it is developing a no-cities capability and is planning to avoid cities insofar as possible. The location of its strategic forces will be an important signal of American interest (or lack of interest) in separating strategic and population targets.

A limited counterforce policy on the part of the United States places

---

* According to a press report in July 1961, the American government was then considering a formal proposal to the Soviets that under no circumstances would cities be attacked in the event of central war. (*New York Times*, July 15, 1961, p. 1).

emphasis on the shared interests with the Soviet Union in reducing the level of destruction in the event that war should take place and in reducing the likelihood of a war that neither side wants. The adoption of such a posture, rather than hindering arms control, should open the way for whatever formal and informal arms-control agreements are possible.

# 7

# American Local-Defense Strategy

THE UNITED STATES is faced with a serious threat to its security posed by the Soviet Union and Communist China. While the threat is a multidimensional one, this chapter deals with only one aspect: the role of local defense with ground forces in deterring local aggression and defending local areas should aggression occur. This is not meant to imply that local aggression is necessarily the most important or dangerous part of the conflict, nor that sound military policy by itself is sufficient. However the military problem is a real one—though dealing successfully with the threat and use of force is not by itself adequate, the failure to meet the military challenge may be fatal to the United States and its allies.

There is a difficulty in an attempt to analyze a particular policy problem. Among the major choices which American policy makers must make is that of the allocation of scarce resources and of government expenditures. In order to do this it is necessary to assess the need to prepare not only for local defense, but also for direct Soviet threats against the United States, and to meet other challenges both foreign and domestic. Before one can decide to spend more for local-war forces, for example, it is desirable to have an idea of where else the money might be spent and what the potential gains of alternative uses of the same resources are.* Nevertheless, before overall budget decisions can be made, a detailed understanding of the possible strategies that are available is necessary.

* See Hitch and McKean [116].

### EVALUATING ALTERNATIVE STRATEGIES

In attempting to evaluate the efficacy of alternative military strategies for the defense of third areas, the actions to be deterred must be specified. For what purposes is the United States trying to use or threatening to use military forces? What actions, by whom, does it consider important enough probabilities to worry about and plan for, and for which of these actions does it want to use force or the threat of force?

The answers to these questions are by no means obvious. Much of the dispute over the sufficiency of present American forces for local war and the likelihood of local war in the coming decade is really based on unstated disagreement about the situations for which one proposes to use military force and the definition of "local war." There are thus two questions to be asked. First, what kinds of actions in local areas does the United States wish to deter by force or by the threat of force? And second, for which of these actions is the declaratory or action policy of local defense with ground forces appropriate?

The problem of what actions the United States wants to be in a position to use force or the threat of force against is a difficult one. The United States wants to be able to use force to prevent the overt violation of borders of countries to which it is allied. But in reacting to violence below that level it encounters major difficulties. It is necessary to be clear as to what kinds of actions can be dealt with by the policies to be discussed, and when and how to be prepared to use force and the threat of force against what kinds of actions.

There are two dimensions to the kinds of situations in which the United States would seek to use force or the threat of force. The first dimension is that of the country being threatened. The United States has demonstrated a willingness to use force to defend major allies and an unwillingness to use force to defend nations in the Communist orbit. However there is a vast area in between in which actions have been ambiguous.

The second dimension is that of the nature of the use of force involved, ranging from subtle threats to overt military attack. In terms of major allies the United States wants to be prepared to use force against even relatively subtle threats of the use of force; against countries with which it has no alliance, it is likely to want only to intervene in cases of overt aggression and violation of international law.

Thus the United States in the past has not used and in the future is not likely to want to use force or the threat of force to try to prevent a number of actions by the Soviet Union or China, because they involve a country to which the United States is not committed, because the use of force is not overt enough (or because of some combination of the two), or because the United States lacks the capability. There may well be situations in which the use of force, even against force, cannot be effective (as the French discovered in Algeria). Even if the United States had what many describe as an "adequate" local-war capability, the American government could not or might not intervene in many kinds of situations. The loss of North Vietnam, for example, cannot be attributed to the lack of local-war forces, unless the United States could have used force or the threat of force to prevent the Communist advance. The military requirements for the defense of third areas can only be evaluated by keeping in mind the limits of the situations in which the United States would be prepared, and should be prepared, to use force.

Closely related to the problem of what actions are to be deterred is the question of *whom* to deter. A major aspect of this problem is whether the immediate opponent is the Soviet Union or China. The two countries are likely to have different incentives in particular situations and to be differently affected by particular threats. For example, the threat of the use of tactical or strategic nuclear weapons against the Chinese may in certain circumstances be more effective than a similar threat against the Russians.

There is a further problem of whom one is deterring in terms of local indigenous forces. Limited use of force in local areas is likely in many cases to involve the use of local indigenous Communist forces, either rebels within the country or a neighboring Communist satellite. In these cases, the effectiveness of a deterrent threat against the Soviet Union or China depends on the extent to which these countries, or these bands of rebels, can be controlled directly from Moscow or Peking. In many cases, the Soviet and Chinese leaders will not have complete authority over these troops, and thus their actions will not be as responsive as they might be to American threats. In addition certain kinds of local-war situations are likely to arise relatively spontaneously—for example, a rebellion in East Germany or other parts of the Soviet satellite sytem. The sudden switching of sides of a major force in Laos in 1961 so that the posssibility of a Communist take-over became a serious challenge to the West occurred almost independently of the actions of any Communist group.

All of this suggests that deterrent threats that depend on verbal communications directly to Peking or to Moscow may not be effective. One of the major advantages of deterrence by defense, or what Snyder calls "denial" [277], is that it is more likely to have an effect on the local indigenous forces which may be a major driving force behind the initiation of limited aggression.

Within these limits of actions and actors, what are the kinds of threats to local areas which the United States is likely to face? The threats can be put into three categories. First is what has become known as nuclear blackmail; this is a threat by the Soviet Union to use strategic nuclear forces against a particular country unless that country yields to an ultimatum of the Soviet Union. This threat may be overt or it may be subtly implied in Soviet actions. The Soviets made use of this threat during the U-2 incident in 1960 when they threatened to destroy bases from which any U-2 planes took off. The second category is armed military aggression either by conventional or tactical nuclear forces of the Soviet Union or China. In the third category of threats are those situations in which there is conflict involving force or the threat of force between two local groups—either within a single country or across a temporary or permanent international boundary—one associated with the West and one with the East, in which the United States would want to have a strategy either of overt intervention or of sending supplies to the side allied with the West.

There are then a number of variables which must be taken into consideration in developing a strategy for the defense of local areas against Communist encroachment: what action is being deterred—nuclear blackmail, overt aggression, or more subtle uses of force? Who is being deterred—the Soviet Union, China, or an indigenous Communist force somewhat controlled by the Soviet Union or China? Who is being defended—a country closely allied to the United States, a country loosely associated with the United States, or one to which the United States has no commitment whatever? What degree of military cooperation with the United States is the local country willing to accept? Can other countries be called on to help in the defense of this country? A desirable capability, communication, and action policy for the defense of particular areas must be devised in terms of possible alternative strategies. Obviously, this whole complex of calculations can only be adequately made in terms of a particular country at a particular time. Nevertheless, some general principles about the problem of the defense of third areas, and in particular the role of a ground-defense strategy, can be laid out.

American strategy for dealing with local threats may rely primarily on one of three levels of military capability: American strategic forces, indigenous strategic nuclear forces, and American and indigenous ground-defense forces. Reliance might also be placed on actions in other areas.

## AMERICAN STRATEGIC FORCES

The efficacy of strategies which depend on the use of strategic forces will vary depending on the nature of the strategic balance. Two strategies might be implemented relying mainly on American strategic forces: massive strategic strikes and limited retaliation.

### Massive Strategic Strikes

The policy of a massive strategic strike is the attempt to use strategic force, whose primary role is to deter central war, to deter and to fight local wars. Thus massive retaliation requires a first-strike strategic capability. The force should be invulnerable so it can threaten without bringing on a preemptive attack.

Herman Kahn [136] and others have proposed that the United States aim for a "not-incredible," first-strike capability, that is, a capability which might be used in very dire circumstances, not because one has a high probability of coming off scot-free, but because one emerges with something like two to twenty million casualties. This might be acceptable in retaliation for certain drastic Soviet provocations. However massive retaliation could also rely simply on the threat to unleash a general nuclear war with great destruction for both sides should the Soviet Union or China attack a local area.

The role of local ground forces for this strategy is somewhat complex. The absence of ground forces may make a strategy of massive strategic strikes more credible. If the West has no other means of countering aggression than the use of strategic forces, the threat to use them is more credible. If the United States were really prepared to use strategic forces, there would be no reason to go to the expense of building up local ground forces. There is, however, another side to the argument. The presence of at least some local ground forces, not sufficient to deter a determined aggressor but sufficient to indicate that a war had started, might be an important component of a massive-retaliation policy. Such forces, although they could not prevent successful aggression, would at least make the aggression clearer. On balance the policy of massive retaliation would seem to require at least a small number of ground forces in the area capable of forcing the enemy to undertake overt military aggression.

The theoretical argument of the previous paragraph has been reflected in the NATO discussions over the proper role of the shield in relation to the sword. The question is how can the shield, the NATO ground forces, be used to complement the strategic nuclear forces. If NATO is relying primarily on a massive-retaliation policy, the question of the role of the shield is precisely the one just discussed. That is, what is the proper size, the proper posture, for ground forces when the primary reliance is on the threat to use strategic forces. NATO has in fact considered and discussed several conceivable roles for shield forces. First is the trip-wire concept, that is, a force big enough so that the Russians would have to go to war to seize an area. A somewhat more ambitious task for the shield forces would be the "plate-glass" role, that is, to force the Soviets to start not a small war but a fairly large war if they were going to attack on the European continent. Malcolm Hoag [121], Osgood [226], and others have argued that neither the trip-wire nor the plate-glass concept justifies NATO forces at the level at which they now exist, or at a higher level. And they have urged the explicit adoption of a local-war strategy for NATO.*

## Limited Retaliation

The strategy of limited retaliation as a means of defending local areas depends as does massive retaliation on the use of part of the capability already existing for dealing with the problem of central war. Limited retaliation involves the threat to use one's strategic forces in a limited way as a punishing device in the event of local aggression. As Morton Kaplan has pointed out, the strategy of limited retaliation is most credible and most likely to be successful when both sides have well-protected, second-strike forces. In this case the threat of limited retaliation and the limited use of strategic forces can be carried out without the fear of touching off a preemptive first strike by the other side [139, pp. 6–8].

The declarations which form a part of a strategy of limited retaliation may be general or specific. In an effort to deter aggression in a specific area (for example, Berlin) the United States, if it were employing this strategy, might threaten the destruction of a particular Soviet city or missile base. Alternatively, the general threat of limited retaliation might be made—that the United States is prepared to use its strategic forces in a limited way to retaliate against armed aggression by the Soviet Union or China.

As an action policy the implementing of a limited retaliatory strike is likely to bring corresponding strikes from the enemy. The success of the strategy depends on a willingness to exchange strategic blows against

* For general discussion of NATO local-war strategy, see Hilsman [115], Hoag [120], and Osgood [228].

cities or missile bases and to increase the scale of the use of strategic forces until the enemy is convinced that we are determined to force his withdrawal from the area of local aggression.

The strategy of limited retaliation seems bizarre to most analysts (and *a fortiori* to policy makers) who question the ability of a democracy to implement it. Nevertheless, as strategic forces become less and less vulnerable to a massive first strike, we will have to pay much more serious attention to an evaluation of the role of the strategy of limited retaliation.

Even in the period of American nuclear supremacy, which seems to be coming to an end more slowly than most analysts had expected, American strategic forces were not adequate to deter or deal with various forms of local military action. As the vulnerability of both sides' strategic forces, and particularly the Soviet forces, decreases, strategic forces will become of less and less use in deterring local wars. Neither the danger of central war nor an increase in this danger during a local war can ever be eliminated; but to count on this to deter local aggression in a period of strategic stability seems to be highly questionable. An effective strategic deterring force, then, is a prerequisite for the defense of local areas, but it is clearly not a sufficient capability. Limited retaliation, though it may come to play a role in deterring attacks on local areas or fighting in their defense, will not substitute for a ground-defense capability.

## INDIGENOUS STRATEGIC-FORCE STRATEGIES

The strategies of massive and limited retaliation discussed previously depend on the use of American strategic capability for the defense of third areas. An alternative possibility is to create an indigenous strategic force controlled by a single nation or an alliance. The latter proposal has been suggested only for European defense.*

The policy of massive retaliation by NATO forces assumes that the threat will be more credible if the alliance as a whole has its hand on the strategic trigger. The alliance would have a strategic nuclear capability, although the dimensions of the capability are by no means clear. NATO

* See, for example, the discussion of this possibility at the Princeton Conference on NATO in 1959 [166, *passim*]. The proposal to create a NATO strategic force was made in a report to the State Department in the last months of the Eisenhower administration by a group headed by Robert R. Bowie. At the Nassau Conference in 1962, Britain and the United States proposed the creation of "multilateral" and "multinational" NATO nuclear forces.

cannot conceivably have a "splendid first-strike capability," and therefore the credibility of the threat of massive retaliation would depend
on the willingness to accept large-scale damage to the alliance countries
following the massive strike. The use of a NATO nuclear force is very
unlikely if this depends on the permission of all (or most) of the members of NATO. Alliance strategic forces could be used for limited retaliatory blows as well as for a massive strike. In this case the policy
might be somewhat more credible but would suffer much the same de-
ficiencies as an American limited-retaliation policy.

## National Strategic Forces

The British in the late 1950's attempted to develop a capability for
massive or limited retaliation with their own national strategic forces.
They have recently given up the Blue Streak Missile and while there is
some pretense that they will try to maintain strategic capability with
bombers, within the next decade, even if the Nassau Agreement is
implemented, the British may have effectively surrendered any possibility of having independent national strategic forces. The French
have recently committed themselves to try where the British failed and
have now authorized the development of a strategic striking force as
well as nuclear weapons.

It would be exceedingly difficult for any individual country (other
than the United States or a United Europe) to have a well-protected,
controlled second-strike force. Thus, in attempting to use the threat of
massive or limited retaliation, the local country would subject itself to
the danger of a preemptive strike by the Soviet Union. Should a number
of countries adopt an explicit declaratory policy of massive retaliation
the Soviets might threaten one country. The Soviets might be able to
bluff the single country into submission or might actually go through
with a nuclear exchange which would destroy the country. This would
quickly make it clear to other states that the policy of massive retaliation depending only on their own strategic forces was an untenable one.
Equally, a limited-retaliation strategy in the situation of vulnerability of
strategic forces is not tenable.

## REACTION IN OTHER AREAS

In addition to the threat and use of strategic forces to deter local aggression or to fight in the defense of local areas, or the use of ground

forces to defend against aggression, there is a third general category of methods which might be used to defend third areas. This is the threat of action in another area.

These alternative actions might take a number of forms, including the use of ground forces in another country. The United States might, for example, in consequence of an attack on Quemoy and Matsu, intervene more actively in Vietnam. The United States' defense of Taiwan after the outbreak of the Korean War is another instance of this type of reaction. In this case complementing the attempt to defend on the ground, the United States intervened in another military conflict.

Such actions might run a whole gamut from the outright use of military force to, for example, resuming U-2 flights or other provocative forms of intelligence to more rigorous action on a diplomatic front (for example, the formation of NATO in response to the Communist coup in Czechoslovakia might have suggested to the Russians that actions of this kind were really not worthwhile). Another instance is the threefold rise in the American defense budget following the Korean War suggesting that, even if the Communists succeeded in their local aggression, they might not gain overall if the consequences were a substantial increase in the American defense effort.

## LOCAL DEFENSE WITH GROUND FORCES

The alternative strategies for defense of local areas just discussed have been based essentially on a punishment notion.* Local defense with ground forces involves attempts to deny to the enemy the territory which he is seeking to gain, by direct ground defense of the local area. This strategy might be implemented by indigenous forces, which would attempt by themselves to develop a sufficient capability to defeat a potential Communist attack. Such capability might or might not include tactical nuclear weapons.† This strategy, which would seek to deter war by threatening to defend on the ground, is extremely credible. However, in sharp distinction to massive retaliation, the fact that the policy is credible is not sufficient to deter aggression. The Communists might believe that a state is prepared to oppose its forces and still commit the aggression. For example, the Chinese Communists must have had a good

* For a general discussion of the distinction between deterrence by denial and deterrence by punishment, see Snyder [277, 280].
† This discussion of capability for local ground defense will not deal with the relative merits of a conventional and tactical nuclear capability. This problem was discussed in Chapter 4.

idea that Tibet was prepared to defend itself; China, with its over-whelming military force, nevertheless attacked.

An "adequate" local defense capability would be one which deterred local wars and won those which could not be deterred by fighting directly in the defense of the area attacked. There may be some cases, however, in which the United States fights a war for goals which do not require victory in the local encounter, and there may be some areas in the world where the United States is incapable of winning a local war, or would not want to fight one. But with those points in mind, it remains true, as Kaufmann has stated, that

despite what may be a comparative disadvantage in manpower, the United States should still be able, with the help of indigenous forces, with mobility, well-organized logistical facilities, great conventional firepower, and highly trained central reserves, not merely to match but actually to beat the enemy at this type of game. After all, Greece and Korea are not figments of the imagination [144, p. 122].

The fighting of local wars will require ground forces, particularly in cases in which the United States is opposing an indigenous Communist movement. Perhaps the most crucial requirement for local war is the ability to apply just the level of force necessary to deal with the situation. This may range from simply being able to supply large amounts of military equipment quickly to indigenous forces to a full-scale intervention by several American divisions. The United States should be able to fight with or without particular weapons, including nuclear weapons, with or without the use of particular forces—tactical air forces, and submarines, for example. The military, then, should be in a position to win with a given level of force without finding it necessary to request permission to expand the war in any way. Military forces should also be in a position to expand the war in subtle ways if requested to do so, for example, to use only a few nuclear weapons. The American forces which may be needed to deal with local-war situations should not be assigned high-priority, central-war tasks which would prevent their use during a local crisis. Unless this is done, military leaders in the field will be constrained from committing their forces locally for fear that they will not be able to perform their central-war missions if the local war explodes.

Strategic mobility and readiness have frequently been cited as crucial attributes of a local-war force. Without deprecating the importance of these factors, it may be well to note that in some kinds of local war they will not necessarily be crucial. In conflicts that build up slowly, such as those in Vietnam and Laos, the gradual infiltration of American equipment and possibly troops may be more desirable than a well-publicized quick move. Nevertheless, in many local-war situations, particularly when the war breaks out suddenly or when the tide of battle turns suddenly, mobility and forces ready for action will be indispensable.

Although airlift has frequently been dramatized as the backbone of mobility for military forces, in the long run sealift is equally important. Airlift may be vital for bringing in fighting units within days and hours, but sealift is necessary to transport tanks, heavy artillery, and other equipment which cannot move with air-borne troops. As the war progresses, sealift will perform more and more of the logistic function. It is equally important to have airfields throughout the world on which planes can be landed, as it is to have ports and staging areas for both planes and ships along the way. The prepositioning of military equipment can drastically reduce the required logistic capability in the earlier stages of a war. Mobility of this kind is required partly because in some countries the presence of American troops is unacceptable for political reasons until a period of crisis, and partly because the United States simply cannot afford to station large numbers of troops at all potential areas of warfare. Thus the United States must be in a position to move troops quickly when the need arises.

Although the United States cannot have adequate forces in every possible conflict area, the value of prepositioning American troops should not be overlooked. The Communists have never unleashed overt aggression into areas in which American troops were stationed. The troops in the area are important partly because they provide a means of fighting the war and stabilizing the situation until reinforcements can arrive. They are much more important for what they symbolize—an American commitment to intervene against aggression. They are probably the best means of signaling to the enemy American commitment and determination to intervene. They also make it impossible for the enemy to launch an overt, massive attack without encountering American troops and, in a sense, forcing them into battle. For many political reasons it is impossible and probably inadvisable to station troops in some sensitive countries (for example, Iran) but the psychological value of such troops in areas where the political disadvantages do not seem to outweigh their deterrence value may be significant.

Indigenous forces will probably be a critical part of a ground-war effort virtually anywhere in the world. Balancing the value of well-trained indigenous forces against other political and economic costs and gains, it may not always be advisable to maintain large indigenous armies, but their value must be considered. Indigenous forces can provide the crucial holding operation, which means that when the United States intervenes, the government in power is still the friendly one that the American forces are going to protect. But perhaps more important, indigenous forces provide a vital element of discrimination in the fighting of local wars. If indigenous forces are capable and competent, they provide a means for American intervention by supplies, technicians, training, and so on, which is much less overt, much less likely to lead to the explosion of the war and to involve great domestic and international political costs, than is the actual use of American troops. This was the case in the Taiwan Straits in 1958 and in Vietnam in 1961–1963. Legalistic differences, such as those between intervention with supplies and equipment and intervention with troops, are one element in the process of limiting war. And the ability to make use of this element when the United States wants to may, in some places, be crucial.

## Communication of Intentions

In addition to making decisions on the kind of capability it requires for local defense, the United States must decide what communications channels it should seek to use and what it wants the other side to believe, both before and during a local war.

Before the war the United States must decide what areas it wants to pledge itself to defend and what it should communicate about the action strategy to be implemented.

With a capacity for direct ground defense and for strategic retaliation, the United States has several options. On one extreme the United States could stress its commitment to a policy of local defense, and assert that the United States will defend any area which is attacked at the level of the attack. At the other extreme the United States could refrain from even discussing the possibility of local war, deny that wars can be kept limited, and assert its willingness to use its strategic forces in the event of the use of force by Communist countries. A third course is to maintain an ambiguous policy, stress the existence of capability for both local defense and strategic retaliation, and not indicate in advance which policy will be used by the United States under such circumstances.

The policy of threatening massive retaliation while maintaining adequate local-defense forces probably produces the most effective deterrent against deliberate large-scale aggression. It enhances belief in the threat of massive retaliation to the greatest possible degree while still suggesting to the enemy that even if the United States is bluffing it has an alternative capability with which to intervene.

On the other hand, the specific commitment of the United States to local war may reduce the deterrent threat; the likelihood of the United

States' immediately unleashing a strategic strike would be much lower. However, if war should come about, it should be significantly easier to prevent its expansion or an explosion into central war. If the United States is taking the alternative course of specifically disavowing the possibility of local war, then its intervention in local war may be seen as the beginning of the initiation of strategic war and may lead to a preemptive strike by the Soviet Union.

Thus, in areas and situations in which it is not clear that the United States will necessarily intervene, the threat of massive retaliation, if it proves less credible, may in fact invite aggression. In areas such as Western Europe where American troops are on the defense line, the threat of massive retaliation may be a more effective deterrent.

Even if the United States could convey a single-policy threat to the Communist world, there would be much to be said for a policy of ambiguity. As suggested by John Campbell:

The maximum deterrent effect, then, should come from creating in the minds of the Soviet leadership a mixture of uncertainty and certainty: uncertainty whether a local aggression might not result in general war, and certainty that even if it did not, the United States could and would react with such force locally that it would be clear in advance that aggression would not pay [54, pp. 177–178].

In areas where American intervention is in doubt it might be worth stressing a commitment to local defense which makes more credible the probability of intervention. On the other hand, in areas where intervention is not in doubt, it might be worth stressing the danger of central war.

These comments about communication of intent are directed mainly at local war begun by overt Communist aggression. As has been stressed it is much more difficult to deter subversion, guerrilla warfare, and other less obvious forms of aggression. However the factors already discussed may operate in terms of deterring Soviet or Chinese aid to the local Communist forces. In many cases crises will arise precisely because local Communist forces are beginning to defeat local Western forces. In these cases deterrence may prove to be valueless; the United States may be faced with the necessity of choosing between military action or retreat.

In terms of deterring Communist aggression it is not certain that an explicit American commitment to a local-war strategy is desirable. However, if one considers the domestic political problems of creating an American capability for local war, the need for an explicit adoption of a local-war strategy becomes clear. The United States is unlikely to maintain an adequate local-war capability unless the Administration explicitly announces the adoption of a local-war strategy.

This problem has continually plagued the NATO alliance. On the one hand, NATO leaders have been reluctant to discuss the possibility of local war for fear of reducing the credibility of the strategic shield. On the other hand, they have sought to build up forces to deal with a local war should it break out. While from a purely theoretical point of view the policy sought seems to be an optimum one for deterring the Russians, it is one that a democracy and a coalition of democracies cannot put into effect. Unless NATO explicitly recognizes the possibility of local war, the alliance is not likely to raise the necessary divisions to successfully engage in a local war in Europe.

America's allies are likely to greet an explicit commitment to local war with mixed emotions. On the one hand, it would bring more sharply into focus for them the possibility of wars fought on their soil with both Russia and the United States remaining free of attack, and it may well increase, as they perceive it, the likelihood of war. In Europe, for example, insofar as our NATO allies still believe in the efficiency of our massive-retaliation threats, they are likely not to welcome American explicit adoption of a local-war policy. However, as the threat of a strategic strike becomes less and less credible, they may be more willing to discuss this possibility. On the other hand, to American allies in areas where American intervention is less sure and where the chance of some kind of violence is much higher, for example, in Vietnam, Taiwan, and Iran, an American commitment to a strategy of local war is likely to be seen as increasing substantially the chances of American intervention while not appreciably affecting the likelihood of an outbreak of war.

Once a war breaks out it is important, as Kaufmann [144, p. 123] and Schelling [257, p. 34] have suggested, to keep open the channels of communication. If the United States has formal diplomatic relations with its opponent, there might be value in maintaining the relation. This would not only provide a ready channel of communication between the two sides, but would have symbolic value in that diplomatic relations suggest "both a reluctance to permit the conflict to get out of hand and a willingness always to consider a settlement of the dispute" [144, p. 123]. Though every action of the American government and its communication with other groups will be part of the process by which it communicates with the enemy, there may be value in one formal communication channel which can be used to send solemn and comprehensive declarations of intent. A formal channel would also enable each side to send messages that it would be sure the other side would get. The sender, of course, could not be sure that the message would be believed, but at least it would know that the other side would take the message seriously and would try to comprehend its meaning. A formal communication channel might overcome the fact that the United States would speak with several voices, although it would be a handicap to the United States in that it could not transmit what it wanted to. The enemy who was desperately trying to figure out what this bewildering array of signals meant might also welcome a formal communication channel.

The question remains: what should the United States seek to communicate during a local war? In deciding what to communicate, the United States must weigh two conflicting goals. The first is to make clear its willingness to keep the war local; to indicate that the United States is not about to use its strategic forces or to expand the ground war indefinitely; and to establish the limits which form the boundary conditions of the war. The second function of communication is to convey a seriousness and willingness to expand the war if necessary.

Students of local war who stress the dangers and the difficulties of limiting war tend to argue that the United States should have well-defined objectives. Osgood, for example, stressed the importance of having clearly defined objectives and communicating them to the enemy. He argued that it would be dangerous to give aggressors the impression that our conduct is "reckless, capricious, and unrelated to our words" [223, p. 240].

Closely related to this is the suggestion made by Kaufmann [144] and others that the enemy be given to understand what the necessary conditions for maintaining limitations are and what our reaction would be to various possible enemy actions.

Emphasizing, both to the enemy and to our own people, that we have concrete, well-defined objectives in a war may not be completely contradictory to the approach which suggests putting some stress on the possibility of the war's expanding. Kaufmann, after urging well-defined objectives and an attempt to convey our reasonableness to the enemy, went on to suggest that it would be well to drop some hints that we are not prepared to engage indefinitely in this sort of local war. He wrote: "It will be just as well for the enemy to realize that, despite our better efforts at control, our patience is not inexhaustible" [144, p. 129].

As has been stressed, a dominant component of a local-war situation will always be the possibility of explosion; whatever the United States does, however it attempts to reassure, to stress its desire to limit the war, the threat of central war will always be present. What strategy the United States should follow clearly depends on the nature of the situation and on the importance to the United States of holding the area under attack. But it should be borne in mind that the comparative willingness to take risks may be decisive in a war. Those who advocate the continual stressing of American reasonableness seem to assume implicitly that the Soviets can gain from any expansion of a war and will not do so only if the United States has very limited, concrete objectives and is completely reasonable. They assume that the only reaction to recklessness is corresponding recklessness and expansion of war. But as Schelling has argued [260, pp. 7–8] the proper reaction to the taking of risks may be retreat. Doing things which increase the danger of central war, for example, exploding a nuclear weapon, might be taken as the action of a madman, suggesting that central war is so imminent that one ought to preempt. But they may also be taken as a sign of seriousness, of willingness to take the risk precisely because the area under attack is important and worth fighting for. The United States cannot always afford to appear ready to compromise and to maintain concrete, well-defined objectives. If it is losing, and feels that it cannot afford to lose, the way to signal this to the enemy may be to do something that increases the shared risk of central war or to expand the war to a level at which the United States can win.

While the United States should maintain communications channels with the enemy, no single rule can indicate what should be communicated. At some times reasonableness and concrete specific objectives may be the appropriate things to communicate. At other times and in other places, we should seek to communicate toughness and a willingness to change objectives. Local war is not so fragile that we must always act to reduce the danger of expansion, nor is it ever so stable that we can afford to overlook the destabilizing tendencies of any action we institute.

Given a capability for local ground defense as well as for strategic warfare, a communication policy which stresses the existence of both capabilities, and a willingness to engage in local war, what should American action policy for the defense of third areas be?

### Action Policy

It is much more difficult to lay out even general guide lines for action policy than for capability and communication policy. The latter two attempt to deal with the situation that exists at the time. Action policy deals with a hypothetical situation which will never occur precisely as anticipated in the advance planning. In most situations, however, the United States will not want to unleash a major strategic exchange between itself and the Soviet Union and is likely also to want to refrain from limited strategic strikes, except perhaps in situations in which the Soviet Union carries through threats of nuclear blackmail. The West is probably going to want to meet overt Communist aggression on the ground where it occurs. Only forces that can intervene effectively at a low level can be used in cases of subversion, civil war, and threats of the use of force short of an overt crossing of a national boundary. But for many threats of force, many ambiguous uses of force and some not so ambiguous, the United States will not want to intervene at all. Thus even an effective local-war capability is only of value in situations in which the United States after an assessment of its diplomatic and military burdens decides to intervene or where its existence acts as a deterrent. Many threats may be too ambiguous, too obviously successful, or too near the brink of central war for the United States to be willing to intervene, no matter what its capability and declaratory policies have been.

If the United States decides to intervene in a local war the Administration should be clear as to its objectives in doing so. A dominant American objective in any local war is likely to be to demonstrate to Communist nations as well as to allies and neutrals a willingness to fight, when necessary, to prevent Communist expansion by force. The importance of this demonstration is likely to be greatest in the area close to the battlefield. For example, if the United States intervened in Laos it would be largely motivated by the need to convince Thailand, South Vietnam, and other countries that it was prepared to defend them. While restoring the *status quo ante* or changing it to the West's advantage will always be valuable, the fulfillment of American objectives may not depend directly on success on the battlefield. A willingness to fight in areas where victory is impossible may suggest to our allies an even greater willingness to engage in wars in areas where success is more likely, and American goals may be satisfied by stabilization which involves a modest Communist increase in territory. But there is an additional reason why the fulfillment of these goals may not require success on the battlefield. As Schelling has pointed out:

One of the *purposes* of limited war may be to increase the threat of general war. . . . Limited war also subjects the enemy to a heightened risk of general war. To engage in limited war is to subject the enemy to an increased likelihood that, for reasons that may well be beyond the control of the participants, the sheer dynamics of the situation may lead to general war [260, p. 5 (italics in the original)].

This is not to suggest that the United States should not seek to win the local wars in which it engages or that it should always fight in a way that increases the shared risk of central war. However, despite the best efforts of both sides, a local war may explode. For this reason demonstrating seriousness will be an important objective.

## War-Termination Conditions

The question of what objectives the United States should seek on the battlefield of a local war has produced much controversy. General Douglas MacArthur and others believed that on the battlefield there is no substitute for victory; the United States must be prepared to use all the force necessary to "win" the war. On the other hand, others have argued that the only possible battlefield outcome of a local war is the *status quo ante* or some minor variant of that geographic distribution. Neither of these extremes is necessarily desirable or inevitable.

Korea suggests the limits to the kind of battlefield success that each side could expect in a local war. At one point or another in the war it was conceivable that peace would come with the entire battlefield area (Korea) completely in the hands of one side. The war actually came to an end with something very close to the *status quo ante*, perhaps giving rise to the notion that this was inevitable.

The factors determining whether the United States could expect success on the battlefield are likely to include the relative importance to the two sides of the stakes involved, the relative capacities of the two sides to intervene with local-war capability and strategic forces, and relative will.

It is impossible to have unlimited war-termination objectives in a local war, in the sense of expecting the Chinese or the Russians to surrender unconditionally. However America's goals in a local war could go as far as obtaining the unconditional surrender of the indigenous Communist forces. Nor should the possibility of America's accepting defeat be ruled out. As was suggested earlier some of America's goals in fighting a local war might be satisfied, even though the United States lost some territory. In some situations the United States may not be able to satisfy its objectives.

America's battlefield objectives should remain flexible. Unspecified, nonrigid objectives increase the chances of arriving at an acceptable compromise and eliminate the domestic costs which would stem from a failure to gain a stated objective. The United States should not always increase its battlefield objectives if its forces gain a military victory, but it should recognize that a favorable alteration of the *status quo ante* may be possible and might yield important political advantages. But expanding war-termination objectives is not without risk. The enemy may expand the means it is employing rather than permit the United States to gain its new objective, and America's political-effects objectives in the war may not depend on success on the battlefield. Thus, while the United States should not assume that victory on the battlefield is impossible, neither should it assume that victory is always necessary or possible. Raymond Aron has best summed up the point being stressed here. He warned that Korea might have set a dangerous precedent and went on to say that one should not

fall anew into the error of overlooking the middle road between rigorous limitation of conflict and its indefinite enlargement. In short, we should not confuse the renunciation of total victory with the willingness to call it a draw. Military successes are not excluded by a limitation of the war. It is not impossible to obtain successes on the battle field which could induce the enemy to negotiate without forcing him to capitulate [10, p. 107].

America's war-termination objectives in a local war, then, must be flexible. While the United States should not rule out the possibility of success on the battlefield, neither should it count on it. The Administration will always have to attempt to balance the political value of increased military success with the costs and risks involved.

# Annotated Bibliography

*Note. The items are arranged alphabetically by author. The writings of each author are listed in chronological order. The list contains all public writings on limited war which had come to my attention by September 1962. The annotation is aimed at summarizing dominant themes and original points.*

1. Acheson, Dean, "NATO and Nuclear Weapons," *New Republic*, CXXXVII (Dec. 30, 1957), 14–16.

   An excerpt from the author's *Power and Diplomacy*. Criticizes Kissinger's 1957 notion of nuclear war.

2. Acheson, Dean, *Power and Diplomacy*. Cambridge, Mass.: Harvard University Press, 1958.

   Criticizes the policy of massive retaliation and calls for a conventional capability for the defense of both Europe and the gray areas.

3. "The Age of Total War?" *Army*, VII (February 1957), 12.

   A chart indicating that between 1918 and 1956 there were thirty-seven less-than-total wars.

4. Almond, Gabriel, *The American People & Foreign Policy*. New York: Harcourt Brace & Co., 1950. Reprinted, New York: Frederick A. Praeger, 1960.

The atomic bomb cannot be used "against Communist coups in Eastern Europe, against Communist guerrilla warfare in Greece, or against campaigns of native Communist armies in China or other parts of the Far East."

5. Amme, C. H., Jr., "Musings on the A-bomb," *Marine Corps Gazette*, XL (October 1956), 20–25.

Korea was fought under self-imposed limitations tacitly accepted by the opposing sides. It would be very difficult to keep a nuclear war limited.

6. "Army Operations in Limited War," *Army Information Digest*, XIII (June 1958), 41–48.

While insisting that the Army is maintaining a capacity for conventional war, concentrates mainly on the problems of nuclear war. Stresses the importance of both tactical and strategic mobility.

7. "Army Requirements for Strategic Mobility," *Army Information Digest*, XIII (June 1958), 31–40.

Stresses importance of mobility for Army local-war forces. Airlift must be available to move several divisions within a few weeks. Sealift is also needed to transport tanks and other heavy equipment and to provide most logistic support after the initial airlift. Both present airlift and sealift capacities are inadequate.

8. Aron, Raymond, *The Century of Total War*. Garden City, N. Y.: Doubleday & Co., 1954. Reprinted, Boston: Beacon Press, 1955.

An essay on the military-political crises of the nuclear age. The West is engaged in a "limited war" with Russia and must rebuild its military strength.

9. Aron, Raymond, "A Half-Century of Limited War," *Bulletin of the Atomic Scientists*, XII (April 1956), 99–104.

Atomic equalization will make local war more likely and more stable. The limitation of war is imposed at present not by objectives but by the character of available weapons.

10. Aron, Raymond, "Can War in the Atomic Age Be Limited?" *Confluence*, V (July 1956), 99–114.

Limitation of war is necessary because of the destruction power of thermonuclear explosives. The use of tactical nuclear weapons, which is to the advantage of the West, should not be ruled out, nor should the possibility of altering the *status quo* by military success in a local war.

11. Aron, Raymond, "NATO and the Bomb," *Western World* (June 1957), 11–16.

The existence of thermonuclear weapons makes preparations for local war necessary. Questions the decision to rely on tactical nuclear weapons for local defense.

12. Aron, Raymond, *On War* (translated by Terence Kilmartin). Garden City, N. Y.: Doubleday & Co., 1959.

The West is faced with the choice of trying to make war impossible by the threat of great destruction or distinguishing as much as possible between different types of war in order to limit violence. The "second is right and the first fatal."

13. Atkinson, James D., and Donovan P. Yeuell, "Must We Have World War III?" *U. S. Naval Institute Proceedings*, LXXXII (July 1956), 711–721.

The United States must be prepared to fight and win local wars. The military key to a capability for local war is mobility.

14. "Atomic Weapons and the Korean War," *Bulletin of the Atomic Scientists*, VI (July 1950), 194 and later pages.

It is likely that the coming period will be marked by a series of "small wars" waged by satellite armies. The atomic bomb is of no value in this kind of war. The United States must develop large and adequately equipped, mobile land forces.

15. Baldwin, Hanson W., "Russia Can Be Beaten without A-bomb," *U. S. News & World Report*, XXXVIII (Jan. 14, 1955), 48.

The West can defeat the Soviet Union in a conventional war provided it has limited political objectives and is willing to fight a peripheral war.

16. Baldwin, Hanson W., "Land Power as an Element of National Power," *Army Combat Forces Journal*, VI (January 1956), 16–21.

Stresses the crucial role of land power in local wars.

17. Baldwin, Hanson W., "The New Face of War," *Bulletin of the Atomic Scientists*, XII (May 1956), 153–158.

The United States must have a flexible capability to deal with a wide range of military possibilities, and must be prepared to fight conventionally, although nuclear war may be possible in areas other than Europe.

18. Baldwin, Hanson W., "Limited War," *The Atlantic*, CCIII (May 1959), 35–43.

The lessons of history indicate that wars will continue to occur in the atomic age. Limited and expressed political objectives are necessary to keep a war limited. Though nuclear war in Europe is impossible, the use of nuclear weapons in the defense of Quemoy and Matsu may be effective.

19. Barnett, A. Doak, *Communist China and Asia, Challenge to American Policy*. New York: Harper & Bros. (for the Council on Foreign Relations), 1960.

Communist China is unlikely to initiate overt aggression anywhere in Asia in the near future. The threat is mainly subversion and political pressures.

20. Barnett, Robert W., "Quemoy: The Use and Consequence of Nuclear Deterrence." Cambridge, Mass.: Harvard University, Center for International Affairs, March 1960. Mimeographed.

A case study of the 1958 crisis. Examines the difficulties in communicating a threat and concludes that the threat of the use of nuclear weapons did not play a vital role in the episode.

21. Berger, Carl, *The Korea Knot, A Military-Political History*. Philadelphia: University of Pennsylvania Press, 1957.

A journalistic account of the political aspects of the Korean War.

22. Bernal, J. D., "Disarmament and Limited Nuclear War," *New World Review*, XXVI (January 1958), 30–37.

Western reliance on tactical nuclear weapons makes disarmament negotiations more difficult; limiting war is impossible and the goal must be "a turning away from war."

23. Biörklund, E., "Can War Be Limited?" *Air Power*, VI (Summer 1959), 287–293.

Distinguishes between limits in general war between East and West (which are held to be unlikely) and limits in a local war involving not more than one great power. Geography is the most likely limit. While the use of nuclear weapons for defense should not be ruled out, primary reliance should be placed on conventional forces.

24. Bjelajac, Slavko N., "Unconventional Warfare in the Nuclear Era," *Orbis*, IV (Fall 1960), 323–337.

Stresses the importance of irregular forces in local war. Opposes the use of tactical nuclear weapons.

25. Blackett, Patrick Maynard Stuart, *Atomic Weapons and East-West Relations*. New York: Cambridge University Press, 1956.

Contains summary of official policy of the United States and Britain toward local war and reviews of articles on local war by British and American scholars.

26. Blackett, Patrick Maynard Stuart, "Nuclear Weapons and Defence: Comments on Kissinger, Kennan, and King-Hall," *International Affairs*, XXXIV (October 1958), 421–434.

In a Chatham House address, comments on Kissinger's *Nuclear Weapons and Foreign Policy*. Concentrating on problems of NATO, criticizes the notion of nuclear war and argues that it is neither stable nor advantageous to the West.

27. Blackett, Patrick Maynard Stuart, "Thoughts on British Defence Policy," *New Statesman*, LVIII (Dec. 5, 1959), 783–784 and later pages.

A discussion of the role of tactical nuclear weapons in local war. Urges the West to adopt a conventional strategy and to renounce first use of tactical nuclear weapons.

28. Bloomfield, Lincoln P., *The United Nations and U. S. Foreign Policy: A New Look at the National Interest*. Boston: Little, Brown & Co., 1960.

Total war may result from a deliberate Communist probe or arise out of "diplomacy at the brink." The use of the UN during a local war can serve as a symbol of restraint and the willingness to stop short of central war.

29. Blumenson, Martin, "The Soviet Power Play at Changkufeng," *World Politics*, XII (January 1960), 249–263.

Discusses the war between Japan and Russia in the late 1930's. Japan won in the field but Russia won the war by threatening to enlarge it. Japan, busy with China, could not afford a major war but Russia could. The Soviets skillfully exploited this advantage to gain a limited strategic objective.

30. Bowles, Chester, "Our Present Foreign Policy," *Commonweal*, LX (April 30, 1954), 86–95.

A critique of the policy of massive retaliation. The policy has been and will be effective in Europe, but cannot deter military aggression in the gray areas.

31. Braestrup, Peter, "Limited Wars and the Lessons of Lebanon," *The Reporter*, XX (April 30, 1959), 25–27.

The lessons of Lebanon reveal that the United States is unprepared to fight conventional wars. The landing in Lebanon was delayed by obsolete equipment and lack of airlift. Lebanon revealed the dangers in the extent to which the United States is prepared only for nuclear warfare.

32. Brazier-Creagh, K. R., "Limited War," *Brassy's Annual* (1957), 35–45.

Discusses local war from a British point of view. The stabilizing of the strategic balance will make war in Europe possible. The essential limit is on matériel, but it may also be necessary to limit political goals.

33. Brennan, Donald G., and Morton H. Halperin, "Policy Considerations of a Nuclear Test Ban," in Brennan, ed., *Arms Control, Disarmament, and National Security* (New York: George Braziller, Inc., 1961), 234–266.

A nuclear test ban would be of value partly because it would reduce the likelihood of nuclear weapons' being used in a local war. The use of nuclear weapons is so disadvantageous to the Soviet Union as well as the United States that both may refrain from introducing them.

34. Bretscher, Willy, "The Case for Conventional Armaments," *Orbis*, I (Winter 1958), 435–447.

The coming strategic stalemate would make local war more likely. Nuclear weapons are not suitable for the defense of Europe and hence NATO must build up adequate conventional forces.

35. Brodie, Bernard, "Nuclear Weapons: Strategic or Tactical," *Foreign Affairs*, XXXII (January 1954), 217–229.

Urges careful evaluation of possible strategic and tactical fission weapons. The tactical use of nuclear weapons is likely to be of advantage to the West and hence the West should explore the means of limited use of nuclear weapons.

36. Brodie, Bernard, "Unlimited Weapons and Limited War," *The Reporter*, XI (Nov. 18, 1954), 16–21.

If "total war" is to be avoided, the United States must be prepared to fight "limited wars." A rewriting of an early classified document which was among the first theoretical pieces on this subject.

37. Brodie, Bernard, "Strategy Hits a Dead End," *Harper's Magazine*, CCXI (October 1955), 33–37.

Argues that nuclear war and traditional strategy can no longer be the rational instruments of policy. Hence the need for new (unstated) doctrines for the coming decades.

38. Brodie, Bernard, "Strategy Versus Tactics in a Nuclear Age," *Brassy's Annual* (1956), 144–154.

Nuclear weapons made limiting war necessary and the Korean War made it clear that local wars were possible. Stresses the need to consider what sanctions can keep a war limited.

39. Brodie, Bernard, "Nuclear Weapons and Changing Strategic Outlooks," *Bulletin of the Atomic Scientists*, XIII (February 1957), 56–61.

Anticipates some of the points in the author's *Strategy in the Missile Age*. Urges much greater thinking about the military-political problems of local warfare.

40. Brodie, Bernard, "More about Limited War," *World Politics*, X (October 1957), 112–122.

Anticipates some of the points in the author's *Strategy in the Missile Age*, in particular the notion of local war's depending on a massive hobbling of existing power, and his criticism of the theory of nuclear war.

41. Brodie, Bernard, *The Meaning of Limited War*. RAND RM-2224, July 30, 1958.

Chapter 9 of the author's *Strategy in the Missile Age*.

42. Brodie, Bernard, *Strategy in the Missile Age*. Princeton, N. J.: Princeton University Press, 1959.

Deals mainly with problems of strategic deterrence. Chapter 9 discusses the problems of local war as part of an overall strategy. The need to limit the means forces both sides to seek only limited political goals in warfare. The use of nuclear weapons is not to the advantage of the West and would make the limiting of war much more difficult.

43. Brody, Richard A., "Deterrence Strategies: An Annotated Bibliography," *Journal of Conflict Resolution*, IV (December 1960), 443–457.

After a brief general discussion, summarizes thirty-eight papers on deterrence, many of which deal with local-war problems.

44. Buchan, Alastair, "Their Bomb and Ours," *Encounter*, XII (January 1959), 11–18.

The nuclear stalemate makes "total war" unlikely. The West must prepare for local warfare.

45. Buchan, Alastair, *NATO in the 1960's: The Implications of Interdependence*. New York: Frederick A. Praeger (for the Institute for Strategic Studies), 1960.

> A nuclear war in Europe could not be limited; hence NATO must build up its conventional strength and confine nuclear weapons to use in central war.

46. Bush, Vannevar, *Modern Arms and Free Men*. New York: Simon & Schuster, 1949.

> Predicts that tactical (that is, small) atomic weapons will not be possible.

47. Buzzard, Anthony, et al., *On Limiting Atomic War*. London: Royal Institute of International Affairs, 1956.

> Presents the case for "graduated deterrence" and the use of nuclear weapons in local war. Conventional defense in the gray areas is politically and militarily impossible and the problem is to distinguish between "limited atomic war" and "total war."

48. Buzzard, Anthony, "Massive Retaliation and Graduated Deterrence," *World Politics*, VIII (January 1956), 228–237.

> Compares "graduated deterrence" with massive retaliation but not with a conventional-war strategy. Hence does not deal with vital questions of the relative merits of the latter two strategies. Urges that a distinction between tactical and strategic nuclear weapons be established by the West.

49. Buzzard, Anthony, et al., "The H-Bomb: Massive Retaliation or Graduated Deterrence?" [a symposium], *International Affairs*, XXXII (April 1956), 148–165.

> Text of a discussion at Chatham House. Buzzard presents the case for graduated deterrence, that is, the use of tactical nuclear weapons in all but very small wars. The suggestions for distinguishing between tactical and strategic nuclear weapons parallel those in Kissinger's *Nuclear Weapons and Foreign Policy*.

50. Buzzard, Anthony, et al., "On Limiting Atomic War," *Bulletin of the Atomic Scientists*, XIII (June 1957), 216–232.

> Summary of the pamphlet issued by the Royal Institute of International Affairs [47].

51. Cagle, Malcolm W., "Errors of the Korean War," *U. S. Naval Institute Proceedings*, LXXXIV (March 1958), 31–35.

> Reviews some of the tactical military errors of the Korean War. The

gravest error was the failure to use vigorously the forces at hand to win the war.

52. Cagle, Malcolm W., "Sea Power and Limited War," *U. S. Naval Institute Proceedings*, LXXXIV (July 1958), 23–27.

The Navy will play a dominant role in local wars and must champion preparedness for such wars.

53. Campbell, Angus, et al., *The American Voter*. New York: John Wiley & Sons, 1960.

The American public's dissatisfaction with the conduct of the Korean War was one of the factors leading to Eisenhower's election in 1952. The ending of the war enhanced the Republican image as the party of peace. However Korea did not have a major, long-run impact on the attitude of the electorate.

54. Campbell, John Coert, *Defense of the Middle East: Problems of American Policy*. New York: Harper & Bros. (for the Council on Foreign Relations), 1958.

Local war can best be deterred by creating an uncertainty in Soviet minds as to whether strategic forces will be used in retaliation, but a certainty that the United States would intervene. The United States must maintain a dual capability. Though the possibility of war in the Middle East cannot be ruled out, subversion is much the greater danger.

55. "The Case for Tactical Atomic Weapons," *Army*, VI (March 1956), 24–25.

Presents arguments for the use of nuclear weapons in local war.

56. Chassin, L. M., "Armageddon or Fontenoy?" *Interavia*, XIII (April 1958), 314–317.

Local war is "highly improbable." The only alternative to mutual suicide is conventional war. Thus manned bombers will continue to be needed.

57. Church, A. T., Jr., "Deterrence and Delusion," *Orbis*, III (Summer 1959), 141–153.

Single-purpose strategic forces cannot deter local war. All wars are limited, particularly in terms of intensity, geography, and objectives. Nuclear weapons are unlikely to be suitable for use in most local-war situations.

58. Clausewitz, Karl Von, *On War* (translated by O. J. Matthijs Jolles). New York: Modern Library, 1943.

Three factors moderate war: (1) war is never an isolated act, (2) war does not consist of one blow without duration, (3) the result of war is never absolute.

59. "The Cold War and the Small War," *Time*, LXX (Aug. 26, 1957), 14–15.

A summary and review of Kissinger's *Nuclear Weapons and Foreign Policy*. Accepts the argument made by the military services that they are prepared for local war but praises Kissinger for stressing the need for the United States to be psychologically ready to fight such war.

60. Columbia-Harvard Research Group, *USSR and Eastern Europe*. A study prepared at the request of the Senate Committee on Foreign Relations. 86th Cong., 2nd Sess., Feb. 14, 1960. Washington: Government Printing Office, 1960.

The nuclear stalemate increases the need for weapons and armed forces for local war. In the absence of local-war capabilities, the stable strategic balance will lead to an erosion of the successive frontiers of the non-Communist world, by force or threat of force.

61. Cottrell, Alvin J., and James E. Dougherty, "Nuclear Weapons, Policy and Strategy," *Orbis*, I (Summer 1957), 138–160.

Reviews some of the arguments for and against the use of nuclear weapons and urges the adoption of a flexible operational strategy.

62. Cottrell, Alvin J., and James E. Dougherty, "The Lessons of Korea: War and the Power of Man," *Orbis*, II (Spring 1958), 39–65.

Cites four major American restraints—non-use of Chiang's forces, economic sanctions, operations beyond the Yalu, use of atomic weapons. Criticizes all but the last limit without taking note of any Communist restraints. "Will" is as important as "doctrine" in fighting a local war.

63. Craig, Gordon A., "The Problem of Limited War," *Commentary*, XXV (February 1958), 171–174.

A review of Kissinger's *Nuclear Weapons and Foreign Policy* and Osgood's *Limited War*. Criticizes Kissinger's nuclear-war model, and urges the creation of larger conventional-war forces.

64. Cross, James E., "What Is the Army's Job?" *Military Review*, XXXVI (June 1956), 43–47.

The role of the Army is to fight local wars with weapons dictated by political considerations.

65. Davis, W. V., "The Navy in Limited War," *Ordnance*, XLII (March-April 1958), 802–805.

Emphasis in local war must be placed on the ability to get to the scene quickly and apply appropriate force, with precision, to military targets. The non-use of nuclear weapons is a viable method of limiting war; the Navy is prepared for conventional war.

66. Deutsch, Karl W., "The Impact of Science and Technology on International Politics," *Daedalus*, LXXXVIII (Fall 1959), 669–685.

Argues against the "overestimation of small military elites" which he sees implicit in the notion of American superiority in nuclear war.

67. DeWeerd, H. A., *Some Thoughts on the Problem of Limitations.* RAND (unnumbered), Sept. 13, 1957.

Examines alternative limits on the use of nuclear weapons and presents a proposal to outlaw their use against cities.

68. DeWeerd, H. A., *The Korean War: Political Limitations.* RAND P-2059, Aug. 5, 1960.

The Korean War was an unforeseen development at variance both with Western views and Communist expectations. Domestic political controversy had an effect mainly in arousing fears on the part of American allies. United States policy was guided by the desire to unite the West.

69. Dinerstein, Herbert S., *War and the Soviet Union: Nuclear Weapons and the Revolution in Soviet Military and Political Thinking.* New York: Frederick A. Praeger, 1959.

A treatment of Soviet military doctrine concentrating almost exclusively on the effect of nuclear weapons on Soviet general-war doctrine.

70. Dodd, Thomas J., "The Eight Fallacies of the Nuclear Test Ban," reprinted from the *Congressional Record*, May 12, 1960. Washington: Government Printing Office, 1960.

The signing of a nuclear-test-ban treaty would prevent the development of the neutron bomb and other weapons needed for local war.

71. Dulles, John Foster, "The Evolution of Foreign Policy," *U. S. Department of State Bulletin*, XXX (Jan. 25, 1954), 107–110.

The "massive-retaliation" speech of Secretary of State Dulles in which he announced that America would depend on the power to retaliate in order to deter local aggression.

72. Dulles, John Foster, "Challenge and Response in United States Policy," *Foreign Affairs*, XXXVI (October 1957), 25–43.

Raises the possibility of the use of tactical nuclear weapons in the defense of local areas as an alternative to massive retaliation.

73. "The Dulles Doctrine: 'Instant Retaliation,'" *New Republic*, CXXX (March 29, 1954), 10–14.

Statements by Morgenthau, Stevenson, and Pearson criticizing the strategy of massive retaliation. Stresses the point that the greatest Communist threat is nonmilitary. Nevertheless there is a need for conventional forces to deal with local aggression.

74. Dupuy, T. N., "War without Victory?" *Military Review*, XXXV (March 1956), 28–32.

Although limited political goals may require limited military objectives, in the support of these objectives "every will, effort, and energy must be directed toward victory."

75. Dupuy, T. N., "Can America Fight a Limited Nuclear War?" *Orbis*, V (Spring 1961), 31–42.

Questions the possibility of developing a strategy for fighting a nuclear ground war.

76. Dyson, Freeman J., "The Future Development of Nuclear Weapons," *Foreign Affairs*, XXXVIII (April 1960), 457–464.

The next step in the evolution of nuclear weapons is the development of a fission-free neutron bomb. Such a weapon could have a decisive impact on local warfare.

77. Eliot, George Fielding, "Lessons from Suez," *Ordnance*, XLI (March–April 1957), 787–790.

Suez demonstrates the need for well-trained, mobile nonnuclear combat forces to move quickly in order to gain political objectives in a local war.

78. Eliot, George Fielding, "The Army and Strategic Mobility," *Military Review*, XXXVII (August 1957), 3–10.

Big wars do not "grow" from little ones, but expand only if the combatants want them to. Deterrence of local aggression depends on a known ability to intervene on the ground before the enemy achieves his limited objective.

79. Finne, David D., "A Reply to . . . Alexander de Seversky," *Marine Corps Gazette*, XLIII (May 1959), 14–16.

A reply to an article which argued that SAC effectively deterred local war and that the West could not win local conventional wars.

80. Fisher, Roger, "Constructing Rules That Affect Governments," in Donald G. Brennan, ed., *Arms Control, Disarmament, and National Security* (New York: George Braziller, Inc., 1961), 56–67.

Arms-control rules including rules for conduct in a local war can be established by a variety of means including obeying the rule, articulating the rule, making a unilateral promise, unilaterally limiting capability, and negotiation of mutual obligation.

81. Fisher, Thomas L., " 'Limited War'—What Is It?" *Air University Quarterly Review*, IX (Winter 1957–1958), 127–142.

Reviews the implications of the three limits the author sees as crucial in a local war: objectives, methods (that is, weapons used and strategy), and area.

82. Foreign Policy Research Institute, University of Pennsylvania, *Western Europe*. A study prepared at the request of the Senate Foreign Relations Committee. 86th Cong., 1st Sess., Oct. 15, 1959. Washington: Government Printing Office, 1959.

In order to create a capability for local war, NATO should build up its tactical-nuclear and conventional strength to the point where it can defend Western Europe with or without nuclear weapons.

83. Frisch, David H., ed., *Arms Reduction: Program and Issues.* New York: The Twentieth Century Fund, 1961.

Presents a plan for comprehensive disarmament based on a stabilized-deterrence approach.

84. Furniss, Edgar S., and Gardner Patterson, *NATO: A Critical Appraisal.* Princeton, N. J.: Princeton University Conference on NATO, 1957.

Report of a conference which agreed on the need for conventional "shield" forces to deal with less-than-total military action.

85. Futrell, Robert Frank, *The United States Air Force in Korea 1950–1953.* New York: Duell, Sloan and Pearce, 1961.

Discusses restraints observed by the Air Force during the Korean War and the periods of expansion of military operations.

86. Gallois, Pierre M., "New Teeth for NATO," *Foreign Affairs,* XXXIX (October 1960), 67–80.

> Suggests that the United States provide each NATO country with a nuclear-deterrent force sufficient to inflict damage greater than the value of the country. Force would be held under "dual control" and turned over to the country only when it was threatened.

87. Gallois, Pierre M., *The Balance of Terror: Strategy for the Nuclear Age.* Boston: Houghton Mifflin Co., 1961.

> Existence of low-yield weapons has destroyed the physical discontinuity between nuclear and conventional weapons, and this substantially increases the danger of escalation. Therefore even conventional war between the major powers is very rash and unlikely. The West, if it had had the will, could have used the atomic bomb to great advantage during the Korean War.

88. Gannon, Michael V., "Limited vs. Total War," *Commonweal,* LXVIII (Aug. 22, 1958), 510–513.

> Summarizes briefly the views of Kissinger, Aron, and others. Concludes that conventional forces are necessary to deter and fight wars on the periphery, at the same time leaving the northern hemisphere intact.

89. Garthoff, Raymond L., *Soviet Strategy in the Nuclear Age.* New York: Frederick A. Praeger, 1958.

> There is no serious discussion in Soviet literature of the strategy of local war. Soviet propaganda denies the possibility of local war and, specifically, the possibility of using nuclear weapons in a limited fashion. Nevertheless the Soviets have maintained a capacity for local-conventional and tactical-nuclear warfare.

90. Garthoff, Raymond L., "War and Peace in Soviet Policy," *Russian Review,* XX (April 1961), 121–133.

> The Soviets are unlikely to unleash thermonuclear war without a very low probability of damage, and this does not appear likely. They will use the strategic stalemate to apply political and limited military pressure. "Limited conflicts represent the classic form of Communist military action, for limited objectives, at limited risk."

91. Gavin, James M., "Cavalry, and I Don't Mean Horses," *Harper's Magazine,* CCVIII (April 1954), 54–60.

> Stresses the need for air-mobile infantry troops, particularly for atomic war.

92. Gavin, James M., *War and Peace in the Space Age*. New York: Harper & Bros., 1958.

   A plea for larger local-war forces for the Army.

93. Gavin, James M., "Why Limited War?" *Ordnance*, XLII (March-April 1958), 809–813.

   Army forces for local war must be mobile and equipped with nuclear weapons in every echelon where they can be usefully employed—nuclear weapons of precise yield, small in size where necessary, and in abundance.

94. Gellner, J., "What's Our Line?" *Military Review*, XXXVIII (April 1958), 97–104.

   Local nuclear war is impossible. The West must, and can, develop effective conventional forces.

95. George, Alexander L., "American Policy-Making and the North Korean Aggression," *World Politics*, VII (January 1955), 209–232.

   Examines the American decision to enter the Korean War on the basis of contemporary newspaper accounts. Explores alternative explanations of Soviet behavior and concludes that a mutual understanding of intentions may be vital in limiting war.

96. Glasstone, Samuel, ed., *The Effects of Nuclear Weapons*. Washington: Government Printing Office, 1962.

   An official report of the effects of nuclear weapons.

97. Gordon, Lincoln, "NATO in the Nuclear Age," *Yale Review*, XLVIII (Spring 1959), 321–335.

   A protracted nuclear war in Europe is impossible. NATO forces should be large enough so that with nuclear weapons they could defeat any Soviet conventional attack. This would force the Russians to choose between peace and large-scale nuclear attack.

98. Gouré, Leon, trans., *Soviet Commentary on the Doctrine of Limited Nuclear Wars*. RAND T-82, March 5, 1958.

   Translation of an article in *Red Star* which discusses the causes, courses, and objectives of "small" wars as the theory is being developed by Americans. The article concludes that restricting a war to a certain area is impossible in view of modern warfare methods.

99. Greathouse, Ronald H., "Profile of a Dilemma: Limited Nuclear War," *Marine Corps Gazette*, XLIII (January 1959), 24–26.

Urges the United States to use nuclear weapons in all wars. The use of nuclear weapons does not increase the danger of a local war's exploding into central war.

100. Hadley, Arthur T., "Low-Yield Atomic Weapons: A New Military Dimension," *The Reporter*, XIV (April 19, 1956), 23–25.

Urges the United States to organize a highly mobile nuclear brigade which could move quickly to put out any brush-fire conventional attack.

101. Halle, Louis J., *Choice for Survival*. New York: Harper & Bros., 1958.

War is inevitable because it is the only means of settling international disputes, but war can be kept limited if both sides seek only limited goals. The West should use tactical nuclear weapons. War will be kept limited if both sides make clear their goals and the limits they are observing and threaten to retaliate in kind for any breach of the limits.

102. Halperin, Morton H., "The Gaither Committee and the Policy Process," *World Politics*, XIII (April 1961), 360–384.

A case study of the Gaither Committee and its impact on the policy process. The Gaither Report helped to refocus attention on problems of deterring central war and away from local war.

103. Halperin, Morton H., "Nuclear Weapons and Limited War," *Journal of Conflict Resolution*, V (June 1961), 146–166.

Reviews the public literature on the use of nuclear weapons in local war and examines the arguments for and against their use. The United States should rely primarily on a conventional capability. An earlier version of Chapter 7 of this book.

104. Halperin, Morton H., *A Proposal for a Ban on the Use of Nuclear Weapons*. Washington: Institute for Defense Analyses, Special Studies Group, Study Memorandum No. 4, Oct. 6, 1961.

A formal agreement banning the first use of nuclear weapons will reduce the likelihood of their being used in a local war and is in the interest of the United States.

105. Halperin, Morton H., *Arms Control and Inadvertent General War*. Washington: Institute for Defense Analyses, Special Studies Group, Study Memorandum No. 6, March 10, 1962.

During a local war events which might trigger an inadvertent central war are more likely to occur and if they occur are more likely to lead to central war.

106. Halperin, Morton H., *Limited War: An Essay on the Development of the Theory and an Annotated Bibliography*. Cambridge, Mass.: Harvard University, Center for International Affairs, Occasional Paper No. 3, May 1962.

Traces the evolution of doctrine on local war. Includes an earlier version of this bibliography.

107. Halpern, A. M., and H. B. Fredman, *Communist Strategy in Laos*. RAND RM-2561, June 14, 1960.

A case study of the very low-level local war in Laos in 1959. Examines Communist motives and communications.

108. Hammond, Paul Y., "NSC-68: Prologue to Rearmament," in Warner R. Schilling, Paul Y. Hammond, and Glenn H. Snyder, *Strategy, Politics, and Defense Budgets* (New York: Columbia University Press, 1962), 267–378.

A case study of the preparation and impact of NSC-68, a National Security Council paper which warned of the future danger of local war.

109. Hampton, Ephraim M., "Unlimited Confusion over Limited War," *Air University Quarterly Review*, IX (Spring 1957), 28–47.

Discusses the difficulties of defining and limiting local wars; but concedes the need for both a conventional and a nuclear local-war capability.

110. Hayes, John D., "Peripheral Strategy . . . Littoral Tactics . . . Limited War," *Army Combat Forces Journal*, V (September 1954), 36–39.

The United States must be prepared to fight local wars. It should adopt a strategy concentrated on peripheral warfare, utilizing American naval power.

111. Healey, Denis, "Tactical Atomic Defense," *New Republic*, CXXXIV (Jan. 9, 1956), 8–9.

Proposes "graduated deterrence." Urges the West to establish the distinction between "tactical" and "strategic" nuclear weapons so that "tactical" nuclear weapons can be used in the defense of Europe.

112. Herz, John H., *International Politics in the Atomic Age*. New York: Columbia University Press, 1959.

"Limited war" today, unlike that of the eighteenth century, involves deliberate restraint. If war is to remain limited it must be localized and small.

113. Higgins, Trumbull, *Korea and the Fall of MacArthur: A Précis in Limited War*. New York: Oxford University Press, 1960.

An account of the relations between MacArthur and Washington during the Korean War.

114. Hilsman, Roger, "American Military Policy: The Next Phase," *Current History*, XXXIII (October 1957), 208–215.

The spread of nuclear weapons and hence the nuclearization of local wars is inevitable. This trend will mean that ultimately defense of local areas will rest on indigenous troops equipped with tactical atomic weapons. Although not sanguine about these developments, the author urges that we accept them as inevitable and begin planning for them.

115. Hilsman, Roger, "On NATO Strategy," in Arnold Wolfers, ed., *Alliance Policy in the Cold War* (Baltimore, Md.: Johns Hopkins Press, 1959), 146–183.

Surveys possible strategies for the defense of Europe and concludes that there is a need for an alliance strategic force and a thirty-division conventional capability for local war.

116. Hitch, Charles J., and Roland W. McKean, *The Economics of Defense in the Nuclear Age*. Cambridge, Mass.: Harvard University Press, 1960.

The allocation of resources among various defense expenditures including local defense is a problem requiring the application of economic analysis. Advocates a program budget including a "limited-war" category.

117. Hittle, J. D., "Korea—Back to the Facts of Life," *U. S. Naval Institute Proceedings*, LXXVI (December 1950), 1289–1297.

The Navy as presently constituted is the best possible force for fighting wars of limited objectives.

118. Hoag, Malcolm W., "Is 'Dual' Preparedness More Expensive?" *Bulletin of the Atomic Scientists*, XIII (February 1957), 48–51.

Preparedness for both total nuclear war and conventional war is less expensive than reliance on the strategic deterrent in all cases, because the latter would necessitate expensive civil-defense programs.

119. Hoag, Malcolm W., "NATO: Deterrent or Shield?" *Foreign Affairs*, XXXVI (January 1958), 278–292.

Argues for a conventional NATO shield to fight European wars which SAC keeps limited.

120. Hoag, Malcolm W., "The Place of Limited War in NATO Strategy," in Klaus Knorr, ed., *NATO and American Security* (Princeton, N. J.: Princeton University Press, 1959), 98–126.

Traces NATO strategy on local war and presents a case for a conventional capability and strategy.

121. Hoag, Malcolm W., "What Interdependence for NATO?" *World Politics*, XII (April 1960), 369–390.

Advocates a conventional strategy for Europe.

122. Hoag, Malcolm W., *On Local War Doctrine*. RAND P-2433, August 1961.

Local wars are part of a global contest for prestige. Considers the alternatives of massive retaliation and local defense and stresses the need for the latter strategy. The Soviets face several risks in launching local violence, including local defeat, high economic cost, explosion, Western mobilization, and adverse political effects.

123. Hoerder, G. H., "Nuclear Defense: The Fear of Retaliation and the Danger of 'Nibbling,'" *Army Quarterly*, LXXIX (October 1959), 68–86.

While retaining a capability to fight small, conventional, limited wars, the West should rely primarily on a nuclear limited-war strategy.

124. Hoopes, Townsend, "Overseas Bases in American Strategy," *Foreign Affairs*, XXXVII (October 1958), 69–82.

Argues that overseas bases, while no longer crucial for strategic warfare, contribute to the deterrence of, and American ability to fight, local wars.

125. Howard, Michael, "Strategy in the Nuclear Age," *Royal United Service Institution Journal*, CII (November 1957), 473–482.

A generally favorable review of Kissinger's *Nuclear Weapons and Foreign Policy*. Somewhat skeptical of the possibility of negotiating limits and of the proposal for nuclear war.

126. Hsieh, Alice Langley, *Communist China's Strategy in the Nuclear Era*. Englewood Cliffs, N.J.: Prentice-Hall, 1962.

Traces Communist China's changing appreciation of the impact of nuclear weapons and her effort to adapt to the nuclear-missile age. The Chinese are seeking a nuclear capability and will try to exploit it to secure their foreign-policy objectives.

127. Huntington, Samuel P., *The Soldier and the State: The Theory and Politics of Civil-Military Relations*. Cambridge, Mass.: Harvard University Press, 1957.

Within the framework of a discussion of military decision making, considers policy during the Korean War. Civilian and military leaders in Washington agreed on the need to limit the war; soldiers in the field, the generals, and the public did not.

128. Huntington, Samuel P., "To Choose Peace or War," *U. S. Naval Institute Proceedings*, LXXXIII (April 1957), 359–369.

The United States must be prepared to wage "preventive" local war as well as "defensive" local war. Although preventive "total war" is an act of suicide, the United States must be willing to initiate preventive local wars. Reviews the criteria for deciding when to initiate preventive war.

129. Huntington, Samuel P., *The Common Defense: Strategic Programs in National Politics*. New York: Columbia University Press, 1961.

In the context of of a general discussion of the politics of defense, traces the development of official American policy on local war. Lacking State Department support, the Army was not able to secure acceptance for the need for local-war forces during the Eisenhower administration.

130. Huntington, Samuel P., *Instability at the Non-Strategic Level of Conflict*. Washington: Institute for Defense Analyses, Special Studies Group, Study Memorandum No. 2, Oct. 6, 1961.

During a period of strategic stability, "domestic" (internal) wars are more likely than local interstate wars. Internal wars are unlikely to trigger central war; their initiation is likely to be the result of local pressures and they may end in total victory in the country.

131. Inglis, David, "Tactical Atomic Weapons and the Problem of Ultimate Controls," *Bulletin of the Atomic Scientists*, VIII (March 1952), 79–84.

Notes the existence of small tactical atomic weapons. This implies that stockpiles of strategic weapons are very large. Although the use of nuclear weapons would give the West a tactical advantage in local wars, the integration of nuclear weapons with ground forces would raise serious political obstacles to the control of atomic weapons.

132. *International Security: The Military Aspect*. Report of Panel II of the Special Studies Project of the Rockefeller Brothers Fund. New York: Doubleday & Co., 1958.

Stresses the need for a more versatile and mobile American military force to deal with a gamut of possible local wars.

133. Jackson, Bennett L., "Let's Start with Conventional War," *Army*, VIII (May 1958), 52–55.

A plea for a dual capability. The use of nuclear weapons in local war is not clearly to the advantage of the United States.

134. Jacobson, Harold Karan, "Scholarship and Security Policy: A Review of Recent Literature," *Journal of Conflict Resolution*, III (December 1959), 394–400.

A review of some of the major books on American military policy and some suggestions for future research. Notes the agreement on the need for local-war forces and doctrine.

135. Josephson, Matthew, "Fantasy of Limited War," *The Nation*, CLXXXV (Aug. 31, 1957), 89–91.

An attack on the "limited-war" theories of Osgood and Kissinger. An antimilitaristic piece which pictures limited-war theorists as "liking limited war." Warns that the effects of local war are unpredictable and urges instead the use of diplomacy leading to peace.

136. Kahn, Herman, *On Thermonuclear War*. Princeton, N. J.: Princeton University Press, 1960.

The book is mainly concerned with the problems of central war. Nevertheless, it explores the problems of the defense of local areas and the role of a local-war strategy and capability. A local-war capability must be backed up by a credible first-strike force if it is adequately to deter limited attacks.

137. Kahn, Herman, *The Nature and Feasibility of War and Deterrence*. RAND P-1888-RC, Jan. 20, 1960.

Presents scheme of three types of deterrence. Places local war in "Type III" category, that is, deterrence of minor provocations. Stresses effect of strategic balance. Summary of some points discussed in the author's *On Thermonuclear War*.

138. Kaplan, Morton A., "The Calculus of Nuclear Deterrence," *World Politics*, XI (October 1958), 20–43.

Criticizes most local-war theorists for failure to use any rigorous model. Makes an attempt to develop such a model and concludes that local defense cannot form the basis of a successful strategy. Suggests instead a limited-retaliation policy.

139. Kaplan, Morton A., *The Strategy of Limited Retaliation*. Princeton, N. J.: Princeton University, Center of International Studies, Policy Memorandum No. 19, April 9, 1959.

Discusses the strategy of limited retaliation as an alternative to local defense and massive retaliation. Stresses the effect of the strategic balance on the conduct of both local war and limited retaliation.

140. Katzenbach, Edward L., "The Diplomatic Cost of Military Penny Pinching," *The Reporter*, X (Feb. 2, 1954), 18–21.

The hydrogen bomb makes war more likely in the Far East but not in Europe. The United States should maintain conventional strength to deal with local wars.

141. Katzenbach, Edward L., "The Military Lessons of Suez," *The Reporter*, XV (Nov. 29, 1956), 11–13.

Suez revealed the need for airlift for limited war. The use of even small atomic weapons will produce great destruction.

142. Kaufmann, William W., "The Requirements of Deterrence," in Kaufmann, ed., *Military Policy and National Security* (Princeton, N. J.: Princeton University Press, 1956), 12–38. (Originally published as Memorandum No. 7 of the Princeton Center of International Studies, 1954.)

The "classic" critique of the Dulles massive-retaliation position. Discusses the requirements for a credible deterrent.

143. Kaufmann, William W., ed., *Military Policy and National Security*. Princeton, N. J.: Princeton University Press, 1956.

A collection of essays on American military policy, most of which reflect a belief in the need for a local-war strategy.

144. Kaufmann, William W., "Limited Warfare," in Kaufmann, ed., *Military Policy and National Security* (Princeton, N. J.: Princeton University Press, 1956), 102–136.

One of the first general discussions of the problems of local war. Stresses the political and military prerequisites for a successful American local-war policy.

145. Kaufmann, William W., *Policy Objectives and Military Action in the Korean War*. RAND P-886, June 26, 1956.

Considers the grievances which the military had during the Korean War and the general problem of civil-military relations during local war. If the military would accept the notion that military action in local war is aimed at securing specific, limited political objectives, they could give valuable policy advice. There is a need for civilian contingency planning for local war.

146. Kaufmann, William W., "The Crisis in Military Affairs," *World Politics*, X (July 1958), 579–603.

A very critical review of Kissinger's *Nuclear Weapons and Foreign Policy*. Criticizes in particular the theory of nuclear war.

147. Kecskemeti, Paul, *Strategic Surrender, the Politics of Victory and Defeat*. Stanford, Calif.: Stanford University Press, 1958.

The essential condition for war's remaining limited is the belief by belligerents not satisfied with the outcome that it cannot be improved by expanding the war. "Limited war" in the nuclear age must be "artificial" in that it depends on a decision to do much less than possible from the very beginning of the war.

148. Khrushchev, N. K., speech on January 6, 1961, printed in *Two Communist Manifestoes*. Washington: Washington Center of Foreign Policy Research, 1961.

At present three kinds of wars are possible: world wars, local wars, and wars of liberation. Both world wars and local wars which may develop into nuclear-missile wars must be opposed. Wars of liberation are just and inevitable and must be encouraged.

149. King, James E., Jr., "Nuclear Plenty and Limited War," *Foreign Affairs*, XXXV (January 1957), 238–256.

Argues against the use of nuclear weapons in local war. Their use is not clearly to the advantage of the West and it would be very difficult to keep a nuclear war limited.

150. King, James E., Jr., "Nuclear Weapons and Foreign Policy," *New Republic*, CXXXVII, "I. Limited Defense" (July 1, 1957), 18–21; "II. Limited Annihilation?" (July 15, 1957), 16–18.

Part I of this review of Kissinger's *Nuclear Weapons and Foreign Policy* is highly favorable and endorses the need for an American strategy for local war. Part II is a highly critical discussion of Kissinger's concept of nuclear war.

151. King, James E., Jr., "Deterrence and Limited War," *Army*, VIII (August 1957), 21–26.

"Limited war" involves substantial interests, but not the survival of the major powers, and is one to which neither side is willing to commit more than a fraction of its military resources. A "win" in local war is a gain in the cold-war political balance.

152. King, James E., Jr., "The Rationale of Agreement between Nuclear Powers: A Method of Analysis," in *East-West Negotiations* (Washington: Washington Center of Foreign Policy Research, 1958), Part I, 38–51.

Local war is possible when both sides' objectives are limited and one side's stake is not clearly greater.

153. King, James E., Jr., "Collective Defense: The Military Commitment," in Arnold Wolfers, ed., *Alliance Policy in the Cold War* (Baltimore, Md.: Johns Hopkins Press, 1959), 103–145.

Outlines goals of American alliance policy and sketches its development. Urges the creation of a local-war command and the stationing of United States tactical forces in a central reserve in the United States. Argues for a much larger conventional force to make possible a flexible military policy.

154. King, James E., Jr., "NATO: Genesis, Progress, Problems," in Gordon B. Turner and Richard D. Challener, eds., *National Security in the Nuclear Age* (New York: Frederick A. Praeger, 1960), 143–172.

Urges the creation of larger NATO ground forces, capable of fighting a conventional war but possessing a nuclear capability to deter a Soviet nuclear attack.

155. Kintner, William R., and George C. Reinhardt, *Atomic Weapons in Land Combat.* Harrisburg, Pa.: Military Service Publishing Co., 1953; 2nd ed., 1954.

Essentially a manual for infantry combat. Discusses the effect of the "nominal" 20-kiloton atomic weapon on combat strategy and tactics. Optimistic about the ability of the United States Army to fight and win a land nuclear war.

156. Kissinger, Henry A., "American Policy and Preventive War," *Yale Review*, XLIV (Spring 1955), 321–339.

Rejects preventive war and suggests in broad terms the need for an alternative between peace and total war.

157. Kissinger, Henry A., "Military Policy and Defense of the 'Grey Areas,'" *Foreign Affairs*, XXXIII (April 1955), 416–428.

Anticipates some of the arguments in the author's *Nuclear Weapons and Foreign Policy*. Only hints at the possible role of tactical nuclear weapons in local war.

158. Kissinger, Henry A., "Force and Diplomacy in the Nuclear Age," *Foreign Affairs*, XXXIV (April 1956), 349–366.

Anticipates some of the arguments in the author's *Nuclear Weapons and Foreign Policy*. The use of nuclear weapons is inevitable in any local war. Limited political objectives are needed to keep a war limited.

159. Kissinger, Henry A., *Nuclear Weapons and Foreign Policy*. New York: Harper & Bros. (for the Council on Foreign Relations), 1957.

The most widely read study of local war. Presents the case for a nuclear-war strategy for the United States. Now outdated by changes in the author's views.

160. Kissinger, Henry A., "Strategy and Organization," *Foreign Affairs*, XXXV (April 1957), 379–394.

A war between major powers can remain limited only if at some point one of the protagonists prefers a limited defeat to an additional commitment of resources. Proposes the creation of a tactical force to deal with local wars.

161. Kissinger, Henry A., "Controls, Inspection and Limited War," *The Reporter*, XVI (June 13, 1957), 14–19.

Disarmament negotiations should be used to convey to the enemy the American notion of local war. In this way diplomacy could be related to force, making it more likely that the United States would resist Communist aggression without bringing on "total war." A summary of some of the points made by the author in *Nuclear Weapons and Foreign Policy*.

162. Kissinger, Henry A., "Nuclear Testing and the Problem of Peace," *Foreign Affairs*, XXXVII (October 1958), 1–18.

Stresses the relation between the test-ban negotiations and potential agreement, and the use of nuclear weapons in local war. Urges further testing to develop improved tactical nuclear weapons.

163. Kissinger, Henry A., "Limited War: Nuclear or Conventional?— A Reappraisal," in Donald G. Brennan, ed., *Arms Control, Disarmament and National Security* (New York: George Braziller, Inc., 1961), 138–152. Originally published in *Daedalus*, LXXXIX (Fall 1960), 800–817.

The author reexamines the arguments for and against the use of nuclear weapons in local war and concludes that the United States should place primary reliance on a conventional-war capability.

164. Kissinger, Henry A., *The Necessity for Choice: Prospects of American Foreign Policy*. New York: Harper & Bros., 1961.

Includes the author's reappraisal of nuclear war [163] and a general reevaluation of local war.

165. Knorr, Klaus, *Is the American Defense Effort Enough?* Princeton, N. J.: Princeton University, Center of International Studies, Memorandum No. 14, Dec. 23, 1957.

A general survey of American military policy. The nature of the strategic balance determines the danger of explosion into central war. Stresses great uncertainties facing military planners.

166. Knorr, Klaus, ed., *NATO and American Security*. Princeton, N. J.: Princeton University Press, 1959.

A series of papers and the report of a conference on NATO strategy. Three alternative strategies for the defense of Europe—massive retaliation, limited retaliation, and local defense—are considered. Although there was much disagreement on which single strategy or combination should be adopted, there was overwhelming support at the conference for a conventional, as opposed to a nuclear, local-war strategy.

167. Knorr, Klaus, "NATO Defense in an Uncertain Future," in Knorr, ed., *NATO and American Security* (Princeton, N. J.: Princeton University Press, 1959), 279–306.

With the decline of the credibility of the American strategic threat, the NATO alliance may become most valuable in terms of its local-war strategy. NATO needs a substantial local-war force with a dual capability.

168. Knorr, Klaus and Thornton Read, eds., *Limiting Strategic War*. New York: Frederick A. Praeger, 1962.

A collection of papers exploring various aspects of limited retaliation and controlled central war.

169. Kraft, Joseph, "RAND: Arsenal for Ideas," *Harper's Magazine*, CCXXI (July 1960), 69–76.

Includes a discussion of RAND research on the problems of the vulnerability of American strategic forces.

170. Lapp, Ralph, *The New Force: The Story of Atoms and People*. New York: Harper & Bros., 1953.

Chapter 7 explores the potential battlefield uses of atomic weapons. The only definite conclusion is that tactical atomic weapons can prevent concentration. Traces government policy on battlefield atomic weapons.

171. Larionov, V., "The Doctrine of Aggression in Doses," *Red Star* (July 8, 1959). Translated in *Survival*, I (September–October 1959), 135–136.

A Soviet review of Kissinger's *Nuclear Weapons and Foreign Policy*. The book is seen as an attempt to develop a strategy for the aggressive use of force by the West, in view of the impossibility of launching a successful global war.

172. Larrabee, Eric, "Korea: The Military Lesson," *Harper's Magazine*, CCI (November 1950), 51–57.

"The military lesson" is that the American soldier and the United States Army are overloaded with machines and frills. Wars, like the Korean War, which depend on guerrilla tactics and indigenous support, will be won by foot soldiers and not machines.

173. Leghorn, Richard, "No Need to Bomb Cities to Win War," *U. S. News & World Report*, XXXVIII (Jan. 28, 1955), 78–94.

The West should adopt a nuclear strategy to overcome Communist manpower advantages. The West should use tactical nuclear weapons to meet a conventional attack and a strategic counterforce strike against a nuclear attack.

174. Leites, Nathan, *A Study of Bolshevism*. Glencoe, Ill.: The Free Press, 1957.

Examines the operational code of the Bolsheviks. The code suggests a willingness to engage in limited military actions as well as a compulsion to fill power vacuums, but a fear of adventurous acts.

175. Lemnitzer, Lyman L., "Forward Strategy Reappraised," *Survival*, III (January–February 1961), 22–25.

Local war is more likely than central war. Local war creates two major requirements: quick reaction and the ability to apply the degree of force needed to defeat the enemy without inflicting undue losses on noncombatants or risking general war. Versatile, dual-capable ground forces are needed.

176. Lichterman, Martin, "Korea: Problems in Limited War," in Gordon B. Turner and Richard D. Challener, eds., *National Security in the Nuclear Age* (New York: Frederick A. Praeger, 1960), 31–56.

A case study of policy making during the Korean War. Examines the restraints on both sides and stresses the need for improved civil-military relations.

177. Liddell-Hart, Basil H., "War, Limited," *Harper's Magazine*, CXCII (March 1946), 193–203.

Views limiting war as part of a historical process aimed at making war more humane. Hopes that international agreement will recognize the great destructive power of new weapons and lay down rules for limiting their use.

178. Liddell-Hart, Basil H., *The Revolution in Warfare*. New Haven, Conn.: Yale University Press, 1947.

Since it is likely to prove impossible to eliminate war, the best chance may lie in trying to revive a code of rules for limiting warfare, based on a realistic view that wars are likely to occur again, and that the limitation of their destructiveness is in everybody's interest.

179. Liddell-Hart, Basil H., "Military Strategy vs. Common Sense," *The Saturday Review*, XXXIX (March 3, 1956), 7–8 and later pages.

Urges that NATO develop a conventional force strong enough to defend Europe in the event of attack.

180. Liddell-Hart, Basil H., "Western Defense Planning," *Military Review*, XXXVI (June 1956), 3–10.

The West must be capable of applying the minimum force necessary to repel any particular aggression. The aim of local war is to force the aggressor to abandon his goals. The "safest" form of action is nonnuclear; by solving organizational problems the West can repel aggression with conventional forces.

181. Liddell-Hart, Basil H., *Deterrent or Defense: A Fresh Look at the West's Military Position*. New York: Frederick A. Praeger, 1960.

The use of neither large nor small tactical nuclear weapons would be to the advantage of the West. Twenty-six NATO divisions could defend Europe conventionally.

182. "Limited War: The Prospects and Possibilities," *Army Information Digest*, XIII (June 1958), 6–20.

Local war is possible and depends on maintaining limited objectives. The absolute precondition of local war is the maintenance of a strategic deterrent. The most significant thing about the limits in Korea is that both sides used quite different criteria for limiting operations.

183. "Limited War: Where Do They Stand: Army, Navy, Air Force," *Army-Navy-Air Force Register*, LXXX (May 23, 1959), 24–25.

Statements by Army, Navy, and Air Force spokesmen. The Army and Navy stress the need for local-war forces, the Navy implying that it can do the job alone and the Army stressing the need for contributions from all services. The Air Force argues that forces drawn from the central-war capability can deter and fight local wars.

184. " 'Limited Wars' Need Big Battalions," *Interavia*, XI (October 1956), 773–776.

The threat of using nuclear weapons may help to deter local war. However there are likely to be numerous local wars in which the West would not want to initiate the use of nuclear weapons. Thus large conventional forces are needed.

185. Lincoln, George A., and Amos A. Jordan, Jr., "Limited War and the Scholars," *Military Review*, XXXVII (January 1958), 50–60.

A very favorable review and summary of Osgood's *Limited War* and Kissinger's *Nuclear Weapons and Foreign Policy*. Supports Osgood on the need for a dual capability and the possibility of conventional war in Europe.

186. Lincoln, George A., and Amos A. Jordan, Jr., "Technology and the Changing Nature of General War," *Military Review*, XXXVII (May 1957), 3–13.

Local war does not lend itself to precise planning; it is not consistent with American temperament and not suited to the American political system. Nevertheless the United States needs the means for local war.

187. Lippmann, Walter, *The Communist World and Ours*. Boston: Little, Brown & Co., 1958.

Based on a visit to the Soviet Union and an interview with Khrushchev. The Soviets genuinely fear a Western military attack. Though the West must maintain its military strength, the real struggle is ideological and economic.

188. Lyman, Princeton Nathan, "Alliances and the Defense of Southeast Asia: A Study of American Policy in Southeast Asia 1950–1960," unpublished doctoral dissertation, Harvard University, May 1961.

Includes a case study of the American decision not to intervene in Indochina in 1954.

189. Lyons, Gene M., *Military Policy and Economic Aid: The Korean Case, 1950–1953*. Columbus: Ohio State University Press, 1961.

Traces the conflict between political and military control of relief and reconstruction in Korea during the war. Criticizes the failure of American officials to prevent military domination.

190. McIntyre, William R., "Limited War," *Editorial Research Reports*, II (July 23, 1958), 549–568.

Surveys official policy, service attitudes, and the public literature on local war. Points out the substantial agreement in the literature on the requirements for local war.

191. Mackay, K., "The Graduated Deterrent," *Military Review*, XXXVII (January 1958), 78–84.

The West should use sufficient nuclear power and widen the area of conflict sufficiently to restore the *status quo* after a limited aggression.

192. McNamara, Robert S., "Defense Arrangements of the North Atlantic Community," *Department of State Bulletin*, XLVII (July 9, 1962), 64–69.

The speech in which Secretary of Defense McNamara announced that the principal military objective of the United States in the event of central war would be "the destruction of the enemy's military forces, not of his civilian population."

193. Magathan, Wallace C., "How New Would a Modern War Be?" *Military Review*, XXXVI (December 1956), 10–16.

Tactical nuclear weapons should be used in local wars whenever their use is to the military advantage of the United States.

194. Magathan, Wallace C., "Warfare Tomorrow," *Ordnance*, XLI (May–June 1957), 956–959.

General war is likely to remain nonnuclear, but small nuclear weapons may well be used in local conflicts which do not endanger the national existence of either side.

195. *Mao Tse-tung on Guerrilla Warfare*, translated by Samuel B. Griffith. New York: Frederick A. Praeger, 1961.

Mao's classic work on guerrilla warfare which the Chinese Communists hold up as a model for all underdeveloped areas.

196. "In the Matter of J. Robert Oppenheimer," transcript of hearing

before Personnel Security Board, United States Atomic Energy Commission, April 12, 1954 through May 6, 1954. Washington: Government Printing Office, 1954.

Much information on evolving official attitudes toward the role of tactical atomic weapons was revealed during the hearings.

197. Miksche, F. O., *Atomic Weapons and Armies*. New York: Frederick A. Praeger, 1955.

Analyzes some of the battlefield implications of the use of 20-kiloton atomic weapons.

198. Milburn, Thomas W., "What Constitutes Effective Deterrence?" *Journal of Conflict Resolution*, III (June 1959), 138–145.

Suggests combining positive deterrence with negative deterrence to prevent the use of force by the Soviet Union.

199. *Military Situation in the Far East*. Hearings before the Committee on Armed Services and the Committee on Foreign Relations. U. S. Senate, 82nd Cong., 1st Sess., 1951, five parts.

The "MacArthur Hearings" which explore American objectives in the Korean War and the nature of the restraint exercised by both sides.

200. Modelski, George, *The International Relations of Internal War*. Princeton, N. J.: Princeton University, Center of International Studies, Research Monograph No. 11, May 24, 1961.

Other states inevitably are drawn into internal wars because the weaker side seeks outside aid. The success or failure of an internal war is always dependent on the behavior of the international system.

201. Morgenstern, Oskar, *The Question of National Defense*. New York: Random House, 1959.

Places primary emphasis on a discussion of strategic deterrence, and advocates an "oceanic system." Chapter 6 discusses the "Limitation of War" and argues that limited political goals and the strategic stalemate will keep any war from exploding. Urges the use of nuclear weapons in virtually all wars.

202. Morgenstern, Oskar, "The Game Theory in U. S. Strategy," *Fortune*, LX (September 1959), 126–127 and later pages.

A summary of the arguments in the author's *The Question of National Defense*.

203. Morgenthau, Hans J., "Nuclear Weapons and Foreign Policy" [a book review], *American Political Science Review*, LII (September 1958), 842–844.

> A generally favorable review of Kissinger's *Nuclear Weapons and Foreign Policy*. The problems of limiting nuclear war are greater than Kissinger thinks they are; primary reliance should be placed on conventional forces.

204. Morton, Louis, "Historia Mentem Armet: Lessons of the Past," *World Politics*, XII (January 1960), 155–164.

> History is of value in understanding military problems despite the new technology. Reviews the strategy of World War II in the Pacific. Japan failed to assess correctly the requirements and preconditions for the "limited war" she sought to fight in the Pacific.

205. Morton, Louis, "National Policy and Military Strategy," *Virginia Quarterly Review*, XXXVI (Winter 1960), 1–17.

> Drawing on the Korean experience, points out that a local war requires great control over the commander in the field. This control increases the likelihood of disagreement, irritation, and sharp clashes.

206. Morton, Louis, "The Twin Essentials of Limited War," *Army*, XI (January 1961), 47–49; reprinted in *Survival*, III (May–June 1961), 135–138.

> Local war requires both sides to be willing to accept a negotiated settlement and to refrain from using strategic weapons against population centers. A limitation on goals does not guarantee that means will be limited.

207. Murphy, Charles J. V., "Defense: The Converging Decisions: How Much for Which Weapons for Which Services for Which Wars?" *Fortune*, LVIII (October 1958), 119–120 and later pages.

> Outlines negotiations within the executive branch on the allocation of resources between local- and central-war functions.

208. Murray, B. H., "Time for a Change in Our National Strategy to Meet Today's Needs," *Marine Corps Gazette*, XL (November 1956), 44–47.

> Urges the United States to adopt a strategy of local involvement of conventional forces with limited objectives. The Marines must be equipped for and taught to understand local war.

209. Murray, Thomas, *Nuclear Policy for War and Peace*. Cleveland, Ohio: World Publishing Co., 1960.

Urges the United States to develop an arsenal of "tens of thousands" of small tactical nuclear weapons.

210. Nanes, Allan S., "American-Russian Arms Competition," *Current History*, XXXVII (October 1959), 214–221.

A catalogue of Soviet and American capabilities for central and local war.

211. Neustadt, Richard E., *Presidential Power: The Politics of Leadership*. New York: John Wiley & Sons, 1960.

Outlines the shifting American objectives in Korea and the factors (many extraneous to the war) which influenced the changes and the vigor with which the aims of the fighting were pursued.

212. Nickerson, Hoffman, "Limited War 1957," *Ordnance*, XLII (November–December 1957), 428–430.

Opposes the creation of functional commands; favors the use of nuclear weapons in local war.

213. Niebuhr, Reinhold, *The Structure of Nations and Empires*. New York: Charles Scribner's Sons, 1959.

Devotes a few pages to proposals for local war in a chapter on the cold war. Accepts the possibility of limiting war but argues that local war in Europe and local war with nuclear weapons are both impossible.

214. Niemeyer, Gerhart, "The Probability of War in Our Time," *Orbis*, I (Summer 1957), 161–183.

The goal of a local war is really political control of the area surrounding the battlefield.

215. Nitze, Paul H., "Atoms, Strategy and Policy," *Foreign Affairs*, XXXIV (January 1956), 187–198.

The United States should attempt to deal with local aggression without using nuclear weapons. Attacks on the Soviet Union, if necessary, should be limited to military targets.

216. Nitze, Paul H., "Limited Wars or Massive Retaliation?" *The Reporter*, XVII (Sept. 5, 1957), 40–42.

A review of Kissinger's *Nuclear Weapons and Foreign Policy*. Criticizes Kissinger's doctrine of nuclear war and argues that the notion of "limited war" is not a new one. The author traces it back to NSC-68 in 1950.

217. Nitze, Paul H., "An Alternative Nuclear Policy as a Base for Negotiations," in *East-West Negotiations* (Washington: Washington Center of Foreign Policy Research, 1958), Part I, 28–37.

Proposes that nuclear weapons be used only by a country which is attacked and within its own borders. The American strategic force would see to it that the use remained unilateral.

218. Nitze, Paul H., "Symmetry and Intensity of Great Power Involvement in Limited Wars," in *Military Policy Papers,* December 1958 (Washington: Washington Center of Foreign Policy Research, 1958), 55–62.

Develops the concepts of "symmetry" (that is, the level of great-power commitment) and "intensity" (the great-power stake in an area). The crucial limit is that of great-power involvement.

219. Nitze, Paul H., *Political Aspects of a National Strategy.* Washington: Washington Center of Foreign Policy Research, 1960.

Argues the need for a counterforce capability to enable the United States to impose limits in a local war.

220. Norris, John G., "The Nation Lacks a 'Fire Brigade,'" *Army-Navy-Air Force Register,* LXXVII (Oct. 6, 1956), 1 and later pages.

The United States needs a mobile fire brigade to deal with local wars.

221. Ogloblin, Peter, *The Korean War.* Cambridge, Mass.: M.I.T. Center for International Studies, American Project C/58-19, Working Paper III, 1958.

A chronology of the war with some speculation as to Communist motives and a discussion of United States capabilities and strategic objectives.

222. "Organizing and Deploying Our Forces," *Army Information Digest,* XIII (June 1958), 21–30.

Discusses the organization and deployment of Army forces for local war. Stresses the importance of forces stationed in potential local-war areas and the need for forces on a ready alert.

223. Osgood, Robert E., *Limited War: The Challenge to American Strategy.* Chicago: University of Chicago Press, 1957.

Deals mainly with American attitudes toward war and the need to alter the American perspective to accept a local-war strategy. Discusses American military policy in the postwar period.

224. Osgood, Robert E., "Limited War Strategy," *Army*, IX (December 1958), 53–54.

Although the "limited-war" thesis has generally been accepted in principle, American military capability does not reflect this consensus.

225. Osgood, Robert E., "NATO's Strategic Troubles." Chicago: University of Chicago, Center for the Study of Foreign and Military Policy, 1959. Mimeographed.

The value of the NATO alliance will decline significantly unless a local-defense strategy proves feasible. If such a strategy is adopted, it should be reflected in NATO doctrine, forces, and announcements.

226. Osgood, Robert E., "NATO: Problems of Security and Collaboration," *American Political Science Review*, LIV (March 1960), 106–129.

A NATO declaratory policy of conventional war would reduce the deterrent effect of NATO's strategic forces and would be dangerous if not supported by effective capability. Since the NATO countries are unwilling to support large conventional forces, an agreed reduction of NATO and non-NATO forces may be more promising.

227. Osgood, Robert E., "Stabilizing the Military Environment," *American Political Science Review*, LV (March 1961), 24–39.

In the context of a discussion of strategic stability, suggests that deterring and fighting against local aggression will depend increasingly on local defense forces as efforts to increase the stability of the strategic forces are successful.

228. Osgood, Robert E., *NATO: The Entangling Alliance*. Chicago: University of Chicago Press, 1962.

NATO requires an explicit reorientation of its strategy involving a recognition of the need to prepare for large-scale conventional warfare. Traces the evolution of NATO strategy on local defense and the role of tactical nuclear weapons.

229. Page, Thornton, "National Policy and the Army," *Army*, VI (June 1956), 31–33 and later pages.

Local warfare is the only practical military instrument of national power. The Army must be modernized and equipped to play the key role in fighting nuclear wars.

230. Panikkar, Kavalam Madhava, *In Two Chinas: Memoirs of a Diplomat*. London: George Allen & Unwin, 1955.

Written by the Indian ambassador to Communist China during the Korean War, who is clearly sympathetic to the Communist regime. The Chinese decided as early as September 1950 to enter the war if the United States crossed the thirty-eighth parallel. The Chinese were not concerned about the possible American use of nuclear weapons.

231. Pate, R. M., "Danger: Little Wars, but U. S. Is Ready," *U. S. News & World Report*, XLIV (Jan. 10, 1958), 50–54.

The Marine Corps Commandant argues that local war is the most likely kind of warfare. Marines are ready to fight with or without nuclear weapons.

232. "Peace or Piecemeal? The Army's Role in Limited War," *Army Information Digest*, XIII (June 1958).

A special issue of the *Digest* devoted to a discussion of the Army's role in local war.

233. Phillips, Thomas R., "Our Point of No Return," *The Reporter*, XII (Feb. 24, 1955), 14–18.

When American armed forces are equipped to fight with atomic weapons, "then the stage will be reached when war will be only atomic and total."

234. Pickert, General [W.], "The Value of Numbers in the Nuclear Age: I. A German View," *Survival*, III (September–October 1961), 229–233.

Atomic weapons favor the offensive because of the power they give to mobile force. Numerical strength will remain important in atomic war.

235. "The Pistol and the Claw . . . ," *Time*, LXV (Jan. 10, 1955), 16–17.

The article reports that the Pentagon has accepted the notion of the stability of the strategic balance and is planning for little wars based on two requirements: massive airlift and the use of tactical nuclear weapons. Major roles to be played by TAC, naval air power, and indigenous forces.

236. Poats, Rutherford M., *Decision in Korea*. New York: McBride Co., 1954.

Traces the political events of the Korean War.

237. Pool, Ithiel de Sola, "On Escalation and Arms Control," Cambridge, Mass.: M.I.T. Center for International Studies, February 1961. Mimeographed.

Explores motives for expansion. Discusses three levels: the objective situation, the perceived situation, perception of the opponent's perceived situation. Expansion will occur if either side feels it can gain by it, taking into consideration the likely reaction of the other side.

238. Quandt, Richard E., "On the Use of Game Models in Theories of International Relations, *World Politics*, XIV (October 1961), 69–76.

Argues that Schelling's bargaining model [257] is of limited value because it is "far removed from the realities of international relations."

239. Railsback, E. H., "Let's Face It," *Marine Corps Gazette*, XLII (November 1958), 52–60.

The Navy Amphibious Task Force is the only truly integrated force capable of meeting all the initial requirements for local war.

240. Rand, H. P., "A United States Counteraggression Force," *Military Review*, XXXIX (July 1959), 50–55.

American forces in the potential combat area are the most effective deterrent to war. Urges the creation of a joint local-war command including six army divisions and airlift capability for two divisions.

241. Rathjens, George W., Jr., "Notes on the Military Problems of Europe," *World Politics*, X (January 1958), 182–201.

Limits in a local war must be unambiguous. In order for the United States to keep wars limited it must be superior to the enemy at all greater levels of violence. Explores alternative methods for deterring war in Europe and argues that independent nuclear capabilities are likely to be most effective.

242. Read, Thornton, *A Proposal to Neutralize Nuclear Weapons*. Princeton, N. J.: Princeton University, Center of International Studies, Policy Memorandum No. 22, Dec. 15, 1960.

The spread of nuclear weapons and their use in local war is not to the advantage of the West. Hence it should work for the adoption of the comprehensive arms control plan to neutralize nuclear weapons which is presented.

243. "Readiness for the Little War: Optimum 'Integrated Strategy,'" *Military Review*, XXXVII (April 1957), 14–26; *ibid.*, "A Strategic Security Force" (May 1957), 14–21.

Report of a study, by a group of Army officers, of the danger of local war. Proposes the creation of a Strategic Security Force to fight peripheral wars. The best deterrent is American troops on the defense line backed up by a mobile reserve.

244. Reid, William R., "Tactical Air in Limited War," *Air University Quarterly Review*, VIII (Spring 1956), 40–48.

Tactical air was not completely effective in Korea as it operated under political "mismanagement" which imposed restrictions. If properly used it can be decisive.

245. Reinhardt, George C., "Notes on the Tactical Employment of Atomic Weapons," *Military Review*, XXXII (September 1952), 28–37.

With the end of the scarcity of nuclear material, tactical nuclear weapons can now be produced. Examines tactics for the use of nuclear weapons.

246. Reinhardt, George C., "War without Men," *Army Combat Forces Journal*, V (November 1954), 41–43.

The United States must have a strong, highly mobile force of Army divisions to combat local aggression.

247. Richardson, Robert C., "Do We Need Unlimited Forces for Limited War?" *Air Force*, XLII (March 1959), 53–56.

Local war will best be deterred by a diversified central-war capability and a well-publicized willingness to use it. First-strike counterforce capability will deter local war.

248. Ridgway, Matthew B., "The Communist Threat and the Proper U. S. Strategy," letter to Secretary of Defense Charles E. Wilson, June 27, 1955. Printed in Edgar S. Furniss, ed., *American Military Policy* (New York: Rinehart & Co., 1957), 141–148.

The letter written by Ridgway at the time of his retirement as Army Chief of Staff. Calls for larger local-war forces with emphasis on mobility and an ability to defeat the enemy at the nuclear or nonnuclear level.

249. Roberts, Henry L., *Russia and America: Danger and Prospects*. New York: Harper & Bros. (for the Council on Foreign Relations), 1956. Reprinted New York: New American Library of World Literature, Inc., 1956.

In the framework of a general discussion of Soviet-American relations, considers the relative military strength of the Communist and Western blocs. Without dealing explicitly with the possibilities for local war, urges a flexible American military capability.

250. Rosecrance, R. N., "Can We Limit Nuclear War?" *Military Review*, XXXVIII (March 1959), 51–59.

Examines the arguments for nuclear war and concludes that they have been greatly overstated. Urges the maintenance of dual-purpose forces.

251. Rowen, Henry, *National Security and the American Economy in the 1960's*. Study Paper No. 18, Study of Employment, Growth, and Price Levels, prepared for the Joint Economic Committee, 86th Cong., 2nd Sess., Jan. 30, 1960. Washington: Government Printing Office, 1960.

A review of United States' military goals and possible strategies including a discussion of alternative methods for the "direct defense of peripheral areas." Deals mainly with the question of the possible roles of tactical and strategic nuclear forces. Urges the creation of a strong conventional capability.

252. Rowny, Edward L., "Ground Tactics in an Atomic War," *Army Combat Forces Journal*, V (August 1954), 18–22.

Stresses the importance of speed, mobility, and dispersion in fighting land atomic wars.

253. Sackton, Frank J., "The Changing Nature of War," *Military Review*, XXXIV (November 1954), 52–62.

Explores the battlefield uses of nuclear weapons and concludes that the West will always gain from their use because of its technological superiority.

254. Saundby, Robert, "War—Limited or Unlimited?" *Air Power*, II (January 1955), 100–102.

A plea for limited objectives in any war with the Soviet Union.

255. Saundby, Robert, "The Doctrine of Proportional Force," *Military Review*, XXXVII (October 1957), 84–89.

If the United States has and announces limited objectives there is little danger of a local war's exploding. Therefore the United States can expand the means as much as necessary to achieve her objectives.

256. Saundby, Robert, "Air Power in Limited Wars," *Journal of the the Royal United Service Institution*, CIII (August 1958), 378–387.

Local war is marked by a need to move forces to the scene rapidly and then operate under limits imposed for sound political reasons. The Air Force will play a key role in moving troops and equipment.

257. Schelling, Thomas C., "Bargaining, Communication and Limited War," *Journal of Conflict Resolution,* I (March 1957), 19–36.

Argues that limiting points for local wars must be distinct and obvious.

258. Schelling, Thomas C., "Surprise Attack and Disarmament," in Klaus Knorr, ed., *NATO and American Security* (Princeton, N.J.: Princeton University Press, 1959), 176–208.

Suggests the possibility of arms-control agreements aimed at stabilizing local war. In designing arms-control systems the possible need for the agreement to survive a local war should be kept in mind.

259. Schelling, Thomas C., *Nuclear Weapons and Limited War.* RAND P-1620, Feb. 20, 1959.

Limits must be distinct and obvious to the participants. There is a distinct and obvious break between the use and non-use of nuclear weapons based on a mutual recognition of the convention that they are not used.

260. Schelling, Thomas C., "Limited War," lecture delivered to the National War College, Nov. 18, 1959. Cambridge, Mass.: University, Center for International Affairs, 1959. Mimeographed.

Discusses the relation of the strategic balance to local war. A major deterrent to local war is the fear that it will explode. Hence, if the strategic balance is stable, local war is more likely.

261. Schelling, Thomas C., *The Strategy of Conflict.* Cambridge, Mass.: Harvard University Press, 1960.

Includes, among other things, the author's earlier writings on local war One of the goals of local war is to raise the shared risk of central war. Local war should be fought in a way that keeps the "chance" danger of explosion above zero.

262. Schelling, Thomas C., "Meteors, Mischief, and War," *Bulletin of the Atomic Scientists,* XVI (September 1960), 292–297.

Decisions, not accidents, cause war. A controlled strategic force will reduce the likelihood of inadvertent central war and make possible its limitation.

263. Schelling, Thomas C., "Reciprocal Measures for Arms Stabilization," in Donald G. Brennan, ed., *Arms Control, Disarmament and National Security* (New York: George Braziller, Inc., 1961), 167–186. Originally published in *Daedalus,* LXXXIX (Fall 1960), 892–914.

Tacitly agreed-upon limits in local war can be construed as a kind of informal arms control. The methods of communicating and arriving at tacit limits may be similar to peacetime arms control and local war.

264. Schelling, Thomas C., and Morton H. Halperin, *Strategy and Arms Control*. New York: Twentieth Century Fund, 1961.

Examines the interaction of arms control and local war in the context of a general analysis of arms control. Discusses possible agreements dealing with local war and the evaluation of any agreement in terms of its effect on the local-war balance.

265. Schelling, Thomas C., "Nuclear Strategy in Europe," *World Politics*, XIV (April 1962), 421–432.

A main consequence of local war, and a main purpose for engaging in it, is to raise the risk of central war. An explosion into central war is a greater danger than expansion. The longer a war lasts and the greater the level of violence, the greater is the probability of central war. The introduction of nuclear weapons greatly increases this danger, and focuses attention away from the tactical battlefield.

266. Seim, Harvey B., "The Navy and the 'Fringe' War," *U. S. Naval Institute Proceedings*, LXXVII (August 1951), 835–841.

"Fringe" warfare has these characteristics: it is local but with global implications; each war is fought for limited objectives; relatively small forces are used; the Communists generally use satellite forces; and a variety of military and nonmilitary means are used. Because of these characteristics the Navy must play a dominant role in "fringe" warfare.

267. Seim, Harvey B., "Are We Ready to Wage Limited War?" *U. S. Naval Institute Proceedings*, LXXXVII (March 1961), 27–32.

Neither the American people nor the military is psychologically ready for local war. The President must take the lead in gaining acceptance for the need to fight with restraint and without seeking total victory.

268. Shanley, Thomas J. B., "Non-Nuclear NATO Army," *Army*, XI (December 1960), 29 and later pages.

Neither American strategic power nor tactical nuclear weapons can defend Europe: a strong continental force is needed. A conventional slow war will enable the West's superior long-term mobilization capability to be felt. After building up its conventional strength, NATO should announce that it will not use nuclear weapons first.

269. Sights, Albert P., Jr., "Major Tasks and Military Reorganization," *Air University Quarterly Review*, IX (Winter 1956–1957), 3–26.

Urges a reorganization of the military services along functional lines, including the creation of a local-war force.

270. Slessor, John C., "Has the H-bomb Abolished Total War?" *Air Force*, XXXVII (May 1954), 24–26 and later pages.

The West must be prepared to fight additional "Koreas."

271. Slessor, John C., "Air Power and World Strategy," *Foreign Affairs*, XXXIII (October 1954), 43–53.

Air power is not sufficient to deter or win a local war; hence there is a need for ground forces. However a local war in Europe is impossible.

272. Slessor, John C., "The Great Deterrent and Its Limitations," *Bulletin of the Atomic Scientists*, XII (May 1956), 140–146.

Local war is impossible in Europe. In other areas the West could not respond to aggression by launching "total war"; hence local war is possible. The West should threaten to use (and should use) nuclear weapons in local warfare.

273. Slessor, John C., "Total or Limited War?" lecture to the Army War College, January 1957. Reprinted in his *The Great Deterrent* (London: Cassell & Co., Ltd., 1957), 264–284.

The West should announce in advance that it will meet local aggression with whatever force (including atomic weapons) is necessary. War can remain limited if a really vital issue is not at stake for both sides.

274. Slessor, John C., "Western Strategy in the Nuclear Age," *Orbis*, I (Fall 1957), 357–364.

A review of Kissinger's *Nuclear Weapons and Foreign Policy*. Criticizes Kissinger's image of negotiated limits and his acceptance of the doctrine of graduated deterrence. Only very small conventional wars are feasible in Europe.

275. Slessor, John C., "A New Look at Strategy for the West," *Orbis*, II (Fall 1958), 320–336.

In Europe only very small brush-fire wars are possible, but larger wars are possible in the gray areas.

276. Smith, Dale O., "Air Power in Limited War," *Air Force*, XXXVIII (May 1955), 43–44 and later pages.

Air forces provide the ideal weapon for local war. They should be allowed to use atomic weapons and to bomb all enemy airfields and supply depots used in the war.

277. Snyder, Glenn H., *Deterrence by Denial and Punishment*. (Princeton, N. J.: Princeton University, Center of International Studies, Research Monograph No. 1, Jan. 2, 1959.

A theoretical discussion of the roles of denial (that is, local ground resistance) and punishment (that is, strategic massive or limited strikes) in deterring military action. One of the purposes of fighting local war is to raise the shared risk of central war.

278. Snyder, Glenn H., "Balance of Power in the Missile Age," *Journal of International Affairs*, XIV (1960), 21–34.

Equates the traditional balance of power with the contemporary tactical (that is, local-war) balance and the "balance of terror" with the strategic balance. Discusses the interaction between the two.

279. Snyder, Glenn H., "Deterrence and Power," *Journal of Conflict Resolution*, IV (June 1960), 163–178.

Deterrence operates during a local war to prevent expansion as well as before to prevent initiation. Once the threat of massive retaliation is considered by the opponent to have a very low probability, it will cease to deter.

280. Snyder, Glenn H., *Deterrence and Defense: Toward a Theory of National Security*. Princeton, N. J.: Princeton University Press, 1961.

A conventional local war may be policed by the threat to use nuclear weapons and a nuclear war by the threat of limited retaliation. Local aggression can be deterred by threats of direct denial or punishment. Considers alternative strategies for the defense of Europe including a conventional-defense capability.

281. Snyder, Glenn H., " 'The New Look' of 1953," in Warner R. Schilling, Paul Y. Hammond, and Glenn H. Snyder, *Strategy, Politics, and Defense Budgets* (New York: Columbia University Press, 1962), 379–524.

A case study. The Eisenhower administration's adoption of the "New Look" policy implied an unwillingness to maintain large conventional forces for local war.

282. Spaight, J. M., "Limited and Unlimited War," *Royal Air Force Quarterly*, IV (January 1952), 6–8.

Local wars are likely to be peripheral and neither side will use its full power. They will not involve the survival of a major power.

283. Spanier, John W., *The Truman-MacArthur Controversy and the Korean War.* Cambridge, Mass.: Harvard University Press, 1959.

Analyzes the Truman-MacArthur controversy and American policy during the Korean War with the aim of developing a theory of civil-military relations during a local war.

284. Speier, Hans, "War and Peace," *Man's Right to Knowledge: Second Series* (New York: Columbia University, 1954), 69–77.

A plea for the need for limited "civilized" war if destruction of the earth is to be avoided.

285. Speier, Hans, "Soviet Atomic Blackmail and the North Atlantic Alliance," *World Politics*, IX (October 1955), 307–328.

Examines the effectiveness of the threat to use nuclear weapons in local war. Tactical nuclear weapons cannot be considered "conventional" until they are used in a war.

286. Sprung, G. M. C., "Massive Retaliation, Deterrence, and Brush Fires," *Military Review*, XXXVII (July 1957), 79–82.

A sympathetic review of Kaufmann, ed., *Military Policy and National Security*.

287. Stein, Harold, "Limited War: The Challenge to American Strategy" [a review of Robert E. Osgood's book of that title], *American Political Science Review*, LII (June 1958), 533–535.

Cautions against model building in international politics.

288. Stern, Frederick Martin, "Why We Need a Citizen Army," *New Leader*, XXXVIII (April 18, 1955), 8–10.

Advocates the formation of citizen armies in the West to deal with Communist conventional attacks.

289. Stern, Frederick Martin, *The Citizen Army: Key to Defense in the Atomic Age.* New York: St. Martin's Press, 1957.

A plea for the formation of a citizen army in the United States.

290. Strausz-Hupé, Robert, "Limits of Limited War," *The Reporter*, XVII (Nov. 28, 1957), 30–34.

Local war is not an effective check to Communist probing and subversion. Concedes the need for a capability for conventional and nuclear warfare but argues that the battle will be fought out mainly at the two extremes of subversion and the strategic balance.

291. Strausz-Hupé, Robert, "Nuclear Blackmail and Limited War," *Yale Review*, XLVIII (Winter 1959), 174–181.

Soviet forces are equipped with tactical nuclear weapons and thus conventional war, at least in Europe, is impossible.

292. Szilard, Leo, "Disarmament and the Problem of Peace," *Bulletin of the Atomic Scientists*, XI (October 1955), 297–307.

Atomic war is most likely to come through a local conflict in which Russia and the United States line up on opposite sides and start using atomic weapons in tactical warfare. Discusses "rational demolition," that is, limited strategic strikes against cities, as a means of defending local areas.

293. Taft, Robert A., *A Foreign Policy for Americans*. Garden City, N. Y.: Doubleday & Co., 1952.

American troops should not have been sent to Korea without a declaration of war. The Korean War was the final result of a policy of sympathy toward Communism which guided American policy. The United States should have driven the Chinese out of all of Korea.

294. Talensky, N., "On the Character of Modern War," *International Affairs* (Moscow), X (October 1960), 23–27.

The author, a Russian general, argues that in the present circumstances only global war is possible. Some in the West argue for "limited war" because they are not willing to give up the use of force, but "limited war" will inevitably expand to "total war."

295. Tanham, George K., *Communist Revolutionary Warfare: The Vietminh in Indochina*. New York: Frederick A. Praeger, 1961.

The Indochinese pattern is typical of the Communist method of exploiting and hiding behind national revolutionary movements. This minimizes the risk of American intervention and the possibility of successfully directing nuclear or diplomatic threats against Moscow or Peking.

296. Taylor, John W. R., "The Other Half of the Deterrent," *Air Power*, VI (Spring 1959), 183–189.

Stresses the importance of airlift in fighting local wars.

297. Taylor, Maxwell D., "The Army in the Atomic Age," *Quarter-*

*master Review*, XXXV (January–February 1956), 4 and later pages.

The Army is essential to deter aggression short of "total war." The Army is now coping with the problem of integrating atomic weapons.

298. Taylor, Maxwell D., "On Limited War," *Army Information Digest*, XIII (June 1958), 4–5.

American readiness to fight and win promptly any local war not only discourages limited aggression but is a major deterrent to central war.

299. Taylor, Maxwell D., *The Uncertain Trumpet*. New York: Harper & Bros., 1959.

Recounts Taylor's efforts as Army Chief of Staff to develop a capability for local warfare. Urges the creation of a joint local-war command to plan limited operations and to secure modernized forces with adequate airlift and sealift.

300. Taylor, Maxwell, "Improving Our Capabilities for Limited War," *Army Information Digest*, XIV (February 1959), 2–9.

Presents a program for improving America's local-war forces by modernizing them and making them mobile. Joint planning and training for both conventional and nuclear war should be expanded.

301. Taylor, Maxwell D., "Security Will Not Wait," *Foreign Affairs*, XXXIX (January 1961), 174–184.

Plans are on file in the Pentagon, unapproved for fiscal reasons, covering the requirements for modernization and expansion of forces needed in local war, the requirements of airlift, and the organizational changes needed to improve their readiness. These plans should be put into effect immediately to give the Army a capacity for conventional as well as nuclear war.

302. Teller, Edward, "The Way U. S. Army Would Fight in 'Little Wars,' " *U. S. News & World Report*, XLI (Nov. 9, 1956), 56–59.

The use of nuclear weapons in local war is to the advantage of the West. If tactical nuclear weapons are used properly they will make up for the Communist advantage in other areas.

303. Teller, Edward, "Alternatives for Security," *Foreign Affairs*, XXXVI (January 1958), 201–208.

Argues for a nuclear local-war strategy for the West.

304. Teller, Edward, "The Feasibility of Arms Control and the Princi-

ple of Openness," in Donald G. Brennan, ed., *Arms Control, Disarmament and National Security* (New York: George Braziller, Inc., 1961), 122–137. Originally published in *Daedalus*, LXXXIX (Fall 1960), 781–799.

The use of tactical nuclear weapons is clearly to the interest of the United States in neutralizing Russian advantages of central location, massive conventional manpower, and surprise.

305. Teller, Edward, with Allen Brown, *The Legacy of Hiroshima*. Garden City, N. Y.: Doubleday & Co., 1962.

Nuclear weapons will be used in any local war involving American combat forces; their use will not make an explosion into central war inevitable. Without nuclear weapons the West cannot defend local areas.

306. "This Is a Look at the New 'Atomic' Army . . . ," *U. S. News & World Report*, XLII (Jan. 25, 1957), 50–53.

Discusses the make-up of the "Pentomic" Army Division for tactical nuclear war.

307. Thornton, Thomas Perry, "Peking, Moscow and the Underdeveloped Areas," *World Politics*, XIII (July 1961), 491–504.

The Russians stress the danger of general war arising from a local conflict. The Chinese minimize this danger and stress the many opportunities for aiding revolutionary warfare.

308. Tinch, Clark W., "Quasi-War between Japan and the USSR, 1937–1939," *World Politics*, III (January 1951), 174–199.

Gives an account of the local war between Japan and Russia. America, if it is to meet the Russian challenge adequately, must recognize and be ready to deal with "quasi-war."

309. Tobin, James, "Defense, Dollars, and Doctrines," *Yale Review*, XLVII (Spring 1958), 321–334.

Argues that the United States can "afford" the defense programs—including conventional forces—necessary for American survival.

310. Truman, Harry S, *Memoirs*, Vol. II: *Years of Trial and Hope*. Garden City, N. Y.: Doubleday & Co., 1956.

Includes an account of decision making in relation to the Korean War and a discussion of Truman's objectives in resisting Communist aggression in Korea.

311. Tsou, Tang, *The Embroilment over Quemoy: Mao, Chiang and Dulles.* Salt Lake City: University of Utah, Institute of International Studies, International Study Paper No. 2, 1959.

> A case study of the 1958 Quemoy crisis. Examines Dulles' brink-of-war strategy.

312. Tsou, Tang, "Mao's Limited War in the Taiwan Straits," *Orbis*, III (Fall 1959), 332–350.

> An examination of Chinese strategy in the 1958 Quemoy crisis.

313. Tucker, Robert W., *The Just War: A Study in Contemporary American Doctrine.* Baltimore, Md.: Johns Hopkins Press, 1960.

> American doctrine argues that once war takes place there is no moral imperative or practical means of limiting it. Restraint should be observed only against individuals for humane reasons.

314. "Two Books That Support Our Story," *Army*, VIII (October 1957), 12–13.

> Review of Osgood's *Limited War* and Kissinger's *Nuclear Weapons and Foreign Policy.* Stresses the point made in both books that central-war forces cannot fight local wars and hence there is a need for a modernized mobile army.

315. United States Department of the Army, *Bibliography on Limited War* (PAM 20–60), February 1958. Washington: Government Printing Office, 1958.

> An extensive annotated bibliography.

316. Viccellio, Henry P., "Composite Air Strike Force," *Air University Quarterly Review*, IX (Winter 1956–1957), 27–38.

> Discusses the role of the portion of TAC set aside for local-war operations and argues that it is the major deterrent to local aggression.

317. Walkowicz, T. F., "Counter-force Strategy," *Air Force*, XXXVIII (February 1955), 25–29 and later pages.

> Tactical air forces using nuclear weapons can deter and win local wars.

318. Waltz, Kenneth N., *Man, the State and War: A Theoretical Analysis.* New York: Columbia University Press, 1959.

> An analysis of the causes of war. Examines three images of the cause:

human behavior, the internal structure of states, and international anarchy. Concludes that a synthesis of the three is necessary.

319. Washington Center of Foreign Policy Research, *United States Foreign Policy, Developments in Military Technology and Their Impact on United States Strategy and Foreign Policy*. A study prepared for the Senate Committee on Foreign Relations, 86th Cong., 1st Sess., Dec. 6, 1959. Washington: Government Printing Office, 1959.

The stability of the strategic balance makes local war more likely. Nuclear weapons do not necessarily favor the West, and first reliance should be placed on conventional forces.

320. Watson, Mark S., "Can We Limit an A-war? The Lessons of Sagebrush," *Nation*, CLXXXI (Dec. 24, 1955), 550–551.

Examines the lessons of Sagebrush. Atomic war can easily get out of hand. The United States must be prepared to fight conventional as well as nuclear wars.

321. Weyland, Otto P., "Tactical Airpower—Worldwide," *Air Force*, XXXVIII (July 1955), 38–44.

Tactical airpower plays a dominant role in deterring and fighting peripheral wars.

322. Weyland, Otto P., "Tactical Air Power," *Ordnance*, XLII (March–April 1958), 798–801.

Stresses the importance of TAC in deterring and fighting local wars.

323. Weyland, Otto P., "How TAC Stops Limited War before It Starts," *Armed Forces Management*, V (April 1959), 24–25.

Only TAC can apply force at any point on the globe in a matter of hours. This capability deters local war.

324. Weyland, Otto P., "Air Power in Limited War," *Ordnance*, XLIV (July–August 1959), 40–43.

Describes in general terms the role of TAC in local war. Its primary mission is to serve as a deterrent by its ability to reach the scene in a crisis situation.

325. Wheeler, Earle G., "Strategic Mobility," *Army Information Digest*, XII (January 1957), 3–12.

The Army would be ideally suited to meet and defeat local-war threats if it were provided with adequate airlift.

326. Wheless, H. T., "Air Power and National Security," *Armed Forces Management*, IV (December 1957), 8–9.

The likelihood, scope, and outcome of local conflicts are closely related to the central-war posture of the belligerents. The flexibility of air weapons enables the same forces that are maintained for central war to operate effectively in local conflicts.

327. White, Thomas D., "USAF Doctrine and National Policy," *Air Force*, XLI (January 1958), 47–51.

Central-war forces deter local war, and forces for local war can and should be drawn from the central-war forces. Nuclear air power and indigenous ground forces are sufficient to win any local war.

328. Whiteley, E. A., "Limited War—Brute Force or Subtle Pressure?" *Journal of the Royal United Service Institution*, CIV (August 1959), 315–319.

The United States should try by methods of "inconvenience, dislocation and embarrassment" aimed at the enemy's homeland to bring a local war to an end. At the same time America's limited objectives should be stressed in a psychological and diplomatic campaign.

329. Whiting, Allen S., *China Crosses the Yalu: The Decision to Enter the Korean War*. New York: Macmillan Co., 1960.

An examination of Chinese motives in entering the Korean war and efforts of the Chinese to communicate their intentions.

330. Whitney, Courtney, *MacArthur: His Rendezvous with History*. New York: Alfred A. Knopf, 1956.

Discusses the problems of field commander-JCS relations during the Korean War and presents a case for MacArthur's preferred strategy.

331. Wiant, John, " 'Crisis' Maneuver Shows U. S. Ready," *Army-Navy-Air Force Register*, LXXIX (June 21, 1958), 1–2.

Reports on "the first limited war exercise ever conducted by American forces." Troops in Europe were alerted and ready to be flown to Lebanon for a brush-fire guerrilla war.

332. Williams, Benjamin H., "Some Questions Regarding Limited War," *Social Science*, XXXVI (April 1961), 118–119.

Two tendencies—the epidemic character of war and the intensifying tendency in war—make it extremely risky to count on being able to limit war.

333. Williams, Ralph E., Jr., "The Great Debate: 1954," *U. S. Naval Institute Proceedings*, LXXX (March 1954), 247–255.

Atomic weapons can be used only to neutralize the enemy's atomic capability. The United States must maintain a conventional capability to deal with local war.

334. Willoughby, Charles A., and John Chamberlain, *MacArthur 1941–1951*. New York: McGraw-Hill Co., 1954.

Presents the case for the strategy of "victory" urged by MacArthur in the Korean War.

335. Wohlstetter, Albert, *The Delicate Balance of Terror*, RAND P-1472, December 1958.

The fighting of a local war significantly increases the likelihood of central war both by expansion and explosion. Nuclear weapons should not be used in local war because of the danger of explosion and the fact that it is not to the advantage of the West to use them.

336. Wohlstetter, Albert, "The Delicate Balance of Terror," *Foreign Affairs*, XXXVII (January 1959), 211–234.

An analysis of the problems of maintaining a stable strategic balance. This is a shorter version of the RAND paper [335].

337. Wohlstetter, Albert, "Choosing Policies for Deterrence," in Charles J. Hitch and Roland N. McKean, *The Economics of Defense in the Nuclear Age* (Cambridge, Mass.: Harvard University Press, 1960), 333–357.

A slightly edited reprint of the RAND paper, *The Delicate Balance of Terror* [335].

338. Wohlstetter, Albert, "Nuclear Sharing: NATO and the N + 1 Country," *Foreign Affairs*, XXXIX (April 1961), 355–387.

NATO should continue to rely exclusively on the United States for its nuclear strength. One of the principal reasons for opposing nuclear sharing is connected with the need to try to limit a conventional or nuclear war.

339. Wolfers, Arnold, "Could a War in Europe Be Limited?" *Yale Review*, XLV (Winter 1956), 214–228.

Argues that a war in Europe between Russia and NATO can remain limited in that both sides are likely to refrain from bombing industrial centers and cities.

340. Wolfers, Arnold, "Europe and the NATO Shield," *International Organization*, XII (Autumn 1958), 425–439.

Urges the development of a NATO shield large enough to fight a conventional war in Europe.

341. Wolfers, Arnold, ed., *Alliance Policy in the Cold War*. Baltimore, Md.: Johns Hopkins Press, 1959.

A collection of essays on various problems of alliances in the nuclear-missile age.

342. Zagoria, Donald S., "Sino-Soviet Friction in Underdeveloped Areas," *Problems of Communism*, X (March–April 1961), 1–13.

The Soviets believe that the present strategic situation enables them to prevent local wars and to triumph by peaceful means. The Chinese feel that local wars are now more likely and should be exploited.

343. Zagoria, Donald S., *The Sino-Soviet Conflict, 1956–1961*. Princeton, N. J.: Princeton University Press, 1962.

The Chinese are more anxious than the Soviets to support local wars, and argue that the Soviets overestimate the danger of an explosion into central war. Describes Sino-Soviet conflict over support in various local-war situations.

BOOKS PREPARED UNDER THE AUSPICES
OF THE CENTER FOR INTERNATIONAL AFFAIRS

*The Soviet Bloc: Unity and Conflict,* Zbigniew K. Brezinski (jointly with Russian Research Center). Harvard University Press, 1960.

*The Necessity for Choice: Prospects of American Foreign Policy,* Henry A. Kissinger. Harper & Brothers, 1961.

*Strategy and Arms Control,* Thomas C. Schelling and Morton H. Halperin. Twentieth Century Fund, 1961.

*Rift and Revolt in Hungary: Nationalism versus Communism,* Ferenc A. Váli. Harvard University Press, 1961.

*United States Manufacturing Investment in Brazil: The Impact of Brazilian Government Policies, 1946–1960,* Lincoln Gordon and Engelbert L. Grommers. Harvard Business School, 1962.

*The Economy of Cyprus,* A. J. Meyer with Simos Vassiliou (jointly with Center for Middle Eastern Studies). Harvard University Press 1962.

*Entrepreneurs of Lebanon: The Role of the Business Leader in a Developing Economy,* Yusif A. Sayigh (jointly with Center for Middle Eastern Studies). Harvard University Press, 1962.

*Communist China 1955–1959: Policy Documents with Analysis,* with a foreword by Robert R. Bowie and John K. Fairbank (jointly with East Asian Research Center). Harvard University Press, 1962.

*In Search of France*, Stanley Hoffmann, Charles P. Kindleberger, Laurence Wylie, Jesse R. Pitts, Jean-Baptiste Duroselle, and François Goguel. Harvard University Press, 1963.

*The Dilemma of Mexico's Economic Development*, Raymond Vernon. Harvard University Press, 1963.

*Somali Nationalism*, Saadia Touval. Harvard University Press, 1963.

*The Arms Debate*, Robert A. Levine. Harvard University Press, 1963.

# Index